PS-ALGOL IMPLEMENTATIONS
Applications in Persistent
Object-Oriented Programming

ELLIS HORWOOD SERIES IN COMPUTERS AND THEIR APPLICATIONS
Series Editor: IAN CHIVERS, The Computer Centre, King's College, London, and formerly Senior Programmer and Analyst, Imperial College of Science and Technology, University of London

Abramsky, S. & Hankin, C.J.	ABSTRACT INTERPRETATION OF DECLARATIVE LANGUAGES
Alexander, H.	FORMALLY-BASED TOOLS AND TECHNIQUES FOR HUMAN–COMPUTER DIALOGUES
Atherton, R.	STRUCTURED PROGRAMMING WITH BBC BASIC
Atherton, R.	STRUCTURED PROGRAMMING WITH COMAL
Baeza-Yates, R.A.	TEXT SEARCHING ALGORITHMS
Bailey, R.	FUNCTIONAL PROGRAMMING WITH HOPE
Barrett, R., Ramsay, A. & Sloman, A.	POP-11
Berztiss, A.	PROGRAMMING WITH GENERATORS
Bharath, R.	COMPUTERS AND GRAPH THEORY
Bishop, P.	FIFTH GENERATION COMPUTERS
Bullinger, H.-J. & Gunzenhauser, H.	SOFTWARE ERGONOMICS
Burns, A.	NEW INFORMATION TECHNOLOGY
Carberry, J.C.	COBOL
Carlini, U. & Villano, U.	TRANSPUTERS AND PARALLEL ARCHITECTURES
Chivers, I.D.	AN INTRODUCTION TO STANDARD PASCAL
Chivers, I.D.	MODULA 2
Chivers, I.D. & Sleighthome, J.	INTERACTIVE FORTRAN 77
Clark, M.W.	PC-PORTABLE FORTRAN
Clark, M.W.	TEX
Cockshott, W. P.	PS-ALGOL IMPLEMENTATIONS: Applications in Persistent Object-Oriented Programming
Colomb, R.	IMPLEMENTING PERSISTENT PROLOG
Cope, T.	COMPUTING USING BASIC
Curth, M.A. & Edelmann, H.	APL
Dahlstrand, I	SOFTWARE PORTABILITY AND STANDARDS
Dongarra, J., Duff, I., Gaffney, P., & McKee, S.	VECTOR AND PARALLEL COMPUTING
Duan-Zheng, X.	COMPUTERS IN SEQUENTIAL MEDICAL TRIALS
Dunne, P.E.	COMPUTABILITY THEORY
Eastlake, J.J.	A STRUCTURED APPROACH TO COMPUTER STRATEGY
Eisenbach, S.	FUNCTIONAL PROGRAMMING
Ellis, D.	MEDICAL COMPUTING AND APPLICATIONS
Ennals, J.R.	ARTIFICIAL INTELLIGENCE
Ennals, J.R.	BEGINNING MICRO-PROLOG
Ennals, J.R., *et al.*	INFORMATION TECHNOLOGY AND EDUCATION
Filipič, B.	PROLOG USER'S HANDBOOK
Ford, N.	COMPUTER PROGRAMMING LANGUAGES
Guariso, G. & Werthner, H.	ENVIRONMENTAL DECISION SUPPORT SYSTEMS
Harland, D.M.	CONCURRENCY AND PROGRAMMING LANGUAGES
Harland, D.M.	POLYMORPHIC PROGRAMMING LANGUAGES
Harland, D.M.	REKURSIV
Harris, D.J.	DEVELOPING DEDICATED DBASE SYSTEMS
Henshall, J. & Shaw, S.	OSI EXPLAINED, 2nd Edition
Hepburn, P.H.	FURTHER PROGRAMMING IN PROLOG
Hepburn, P.H.	PROGRAMMING IN MICRO-PROLOG MADE SIMPLE
Hill, I.D. & Meek, B.L.	PROGRAMMING LANGUAGE STANDARDISATION
Hirschheim, R., Smithson, S. & Whitehouse, D.	MICROCOMPUTERS AND THE HUMANITIES: Survey and Recommendations
Hutchins, W.J.	MACHINE TRANSLATION
Hutchison, D.	FUNDAMENTALS OF COMPUTER LOGIC
Hutchison, D. & Silvester, P.	COMPUTER LOGIC
Koopman, P.	STACK COMPUTERS
Koskimies, K. & Paaki, J.	AUTOMATING LANGUAGE IMPLEMENTATION
Koster, C.H.A.	TOP-DOWN PROGRAMMING WITH ELAN
Last, R.	ARTIFICIAL INTELLIGENCE TECHNIQUES IN LANGUAGE LEARNING
Lester, C.	A PRACTICAL APPROACH TO DATA STRUCTURES
Lucas, R.	DATABASE APPLICATIONS USING PROLOG
Lucas, A.	DESKTOP PUBLISHING
Maddix, F. & Morgan, G.	SYSTEMS SOFTWARE
Matthews, J.L.	FORTH
Millington, D.	SYSTEMS ANALYSIS AND DESIGN FOR COMPUTER APPLICATIONS
Moseley, L.G., Sharp, J.A. & Salenieks, P.	PASCAL IN PRACTICE
Moylan, P.	ASSEMBLY LANGUAGE FOR ENGINEERS
Narayanan, A. & Sharkey, N.E.	AN INTRODUCTION TO LISP
Parrington, N. & Roper, M.	UNDERSTANDING SOFTWARE TESTING
Paterson, A.	OFFICE SYSTEMS
Phillips, C. & Cornelius, B.J.	COMPUTATIONAL NUMERICAL METHODS
Rahtz, S.P.Q.	INFORMATION TECHNOLOGY IN THE HUMANITIES
Ramsden, E.	MICROCOMPUTERS IN EDUCATION 2

Series continued at back of book

PS-ALGOL IMPLEMENTATIONS
Applications in Persistent Object-Oriented Programming

W. PAUL COCKSHOTT
Computer Science Department
University of Strathclyde

ELLIS HORWOOD
NEW YORK LONDON TORONTO SYDNEY TOKYO SINGAPORE

First published in 1990 by
ELLIS HORWOOD LIMITED
Market Cross House, Cooper Street,
Chichester, West Sussex, PO19 1EB, England

A division of
Simon & Schuster International Group

© Ellis Horwood Limited, 1990

All rights reserved. No part of this publication may be
reproduced, stored in a retrieval system, or transmitted,
in any form, or by any means, electronic, mechanical,
photocopying, recording or otherwise, without the prior
permission in writing, from the publisher

Printed and bound in Great Britain
by Hartnolls, Bodmin

British Library Cataloguing in Publication Data

Cockshott, W. Paul
PS-ALGOL implementations: applications in persistent
object-oriented programming. — (Ellis Horwood series in
computers and their applications)
1. Electronic digital computers programming
I. Title
005.13
ISBN 0–13–741190–1

Library of Congress Cataloging-in-Publication Data

Cockshott, W. Paul
PS-ALGOL implementations: applications in persistent
object-oriented programming / W. Paul Cockshott.
p. cm. — (Ellis Horwood series in computers and their
applications)
ISBN 0–13–741190–1
1. Object-oriented programming. 2. ALGOL (computer
program language). I. Title. II. Series: computers and their
applications.
QA76.64.C63   1990
005.13′3–dc20   89–71639
                                                                CIP

Table of Contents

Introduction   1

1   **Store based computation**   **5**
     1.1   Store models   7
     1.2   Secondary storage and termination   10
     1.3   Two cultures   11

2   **Origins and basics**   **19**
     2.1   Orgins of PS-algol   19
     2.2   Basics   24

3   **Maps**   **35**
     3.1   Vectors   38
     3.2   Pntrs   44
     3.3   Tables   45

4	**Graphics types**		**47**
	4.1	Join and combine	48
	4.2	Transformations	49
	4.3	Pixels	50
	4.4	Pixel mapping	52

5	**Databases and persistence**		**53**

6	**The PS-algol abstract machine: scalar variables**		**59**
	6.1	Implementation techniques	59
	6.2	Stores	63
	6.3	Stacks	64

7	**Object store**		**75**
	7.1	P stack	77
	7.2	The volatile heap	78
	7.3	The idea of a persistent identifier	86
	7.4	Modification to garbage collection	89
	7.5	Implementing the commit operation	89
	7.6	The interface to the persistent heap	91

8	**Disk organization**		**93**
	8.1	Implementation of the LR.map	96
	8.2	Class fractions	98
	8.3	Problems with the POMS	99
	8.4	CPOMS	99

9	**First class functions and modular compilation**		**103**
	9.1	S-algol	104
	9.2	PS-algol	108
	9.4	Dynamic linking	113
	9.4	Persistent S-algol linkage	113

Bibliography   **123**

Index   **129**

Introduction

It has been argued that the normal progress of science is a stagnant business. For most of the time, research workers add little bits to the edifice of knowledge. They are like the masons working on a great cathedral. They fill gaps in the masonry, add decorations to the cornices and porticos but leave intact the basic foundations handed down to them by their predecessors. Occasionally, very occasionally there is a radical change. The old building collapses.

Paradigms
The cathedrals of science are its paradigms. They are the fundamental assumptions of a discipline. Like all foundations they determine what can be built on top of them. Even when they have become invisible beneath the detail of subsequent discoveries the paradigms make themselves felt. The paradigms define the limits of the possible, both in the world and in the mind. For the physics of Galileo to displace Aristotle, observation was not enough. A new mode of thought was required to permit the observation to occur.

Computer science, like any other, has its paradigms, and research programs, but it is peculiar in the intimacy of its links with economic life. It has as its object of investigation a product of human industry: the computing machine. Although, at its most theoretical, our science slides by imperceptible stages into mathematics or even physics, the greater part of its effort goes into understanding real computers and their programs.

Without real computers, without their importance to the economy, computer science would be a dry and restricted mathematical speciality, little studied and less heeded. But our peculiar object, which gives us our importance and our funds, allows paradigms to bind us twice. Other science reproduces and embodies its paradigms in textbooks and in the training of its practitioners. We can materialize our paradigms in three other ways: in computer architecture, in operating systems and in programming languages.

It is a common enough observation that for all its technical dynamism, computing is in many ways conservative. FORTRAN and COBOL remain, for all their long history, the most popular programming languages. The language C is growing in popularity with a computational model that amounts to little more than a sugared FORTRAN. The Von Neumann computer still retains its primacy after even more years. These are among our best established paradigms. They are only visible as such because they are being challenged by alternatives. Newer programming languages cast light upon the limitations of FORTRAN. Dataflow and connectionist architectures contend with the old sage.

Until we come across a new paradigm we are not aware of the extent to which the old one influences us. I recall the intrigue I felt on encountering for the first time a language, Algol68, that allowed a program to define its own datatypes. Before then it had never occurred to me that anything more than arrays were needed.

The paradigm of store based computation
The paradigms in computing, are to some extent, an expression of the limits of our technology. The interesting question is if these limits are permanent or just historically contingent. Which of the current paradigms is to be broken will depend upon the extend to which they are 'just in the mind' or are dictated to us by the properties of the world we live in. This is important. The paradigm that I advocate in this book has a store or assignment based semantics, whereas one of the other influential new paradigms, functional programming, eschews assignment and all its works. The persistent programming paradigm is not the same as the Von Neumann one, but has a lot in common with it. Is the Von Neumann paradigm of store based computation just a hang-over from pioneering days?

If it is, then in time we need to change programmers' attitudes by training them in functional programming. If the store based paradigm is supported by no more than mental conservatism and the dead weight of existing designs, then enough effort by hardware designers will give rise to a new generation of Non-Von Neumann machines. If all this is true then there is not much point in advocating a new store based paradigm.

If on the other hand I an right in thinking that the Von Neumann computer with its random access store expresses certain fundamental physical limitations on the process of computation, then what we are in for is not a root and branch rejection of the old paradigm but a more subtle shift.

4 INTRODUCTION

Notation used in this book

BNF
In the text, PS-algol syntax is illustrated in two ways: by examples of PS-algol, and by definitions in modified Backus Naur Form (BNF). BNF is a formal way of specifying grammars for programming languages. It was first used in the 1960 algol-60 report. The syntax of BNF is shown below. A complete syntax for PS-algol is given in Appendix A.

Symbol	Meaning
::=	is defined as
|	or alternatively
[ ]	optionally
*	zero or more repetitions of
< >	these enclose the names of grammar rules

Anything else is part of the syntax being defined, here, PS-algol.

Other notation
The result produced by program fragments is preceded by the metasymbol --> which is not part of the PS-algol itself.

Some program fragments are given in Pascal and some in PS-algol. In both instances when samples of program code are shown, the reserved words are shown in **bold** to distinguish them from user defined words. In the text **bold** letters are also used as syntactic variables representing the set of all possible productions that can occur in some given context. *Italics* are used to denote numerical metavariables that describe the scale of some computing problem or construct.

1

Store based computation

When we talk about computers nowadays we are generally looking at a particular restricted class of machines - the stored program digital computer. There are of course other approaches to making computing machines. One of these, the analogue computer is now outdated and little used. Other possible models have been proposed based upon neural networks. But the technology for these has not yet come about.

A computer is digital if it represents information in terms of a finite alphabet of symbols. These symbols could be the Arabic numerals 0 to 9, the Roman alphabet, Kanji, or a binary alphabet variously denoted as True and False or 0 and 1. What matters is not so much the particular symbols themselves as the fact that they are finite in number and unambiguously distinguishable from one another.

In addition to being able to represent digital information the computer must be able to store information whilst it is being manipulated. A computer store is a module that can be used to hold information. It must have the following attributes:

1. it must be able to exist in a number of different stable states

6 STORE BASED COMPUTATION [Ch.1]

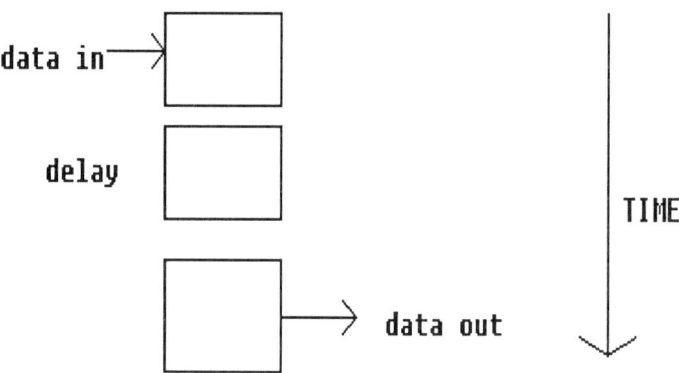

The abstract property of store

Figure 1.1

2. it must be possible to place it in these states using external signals

3. It must be possible to sense its current state.

In mechanical calculating machines the state of the system was stored in the positions of cogwheels or racks. In electronic computers a variety of different technologies have been used. Abstractly all electronic data stores have the structure shown in Figure 1.1.

The minimum property of a digital store is to be able to retain a one or a zero over time. A digital computer capable of performing computation over time must contain a set of storage cells each capable of holding a bit. The computer is capable of existing in a number of distinct states characterized by the set of values in its storage cells. If we consider these we can see that the number of states that the computer can occupy will be 2^s where s is the number of storage cells in the machine.

Computation proceeds by the computer going from one state to the next. Clearly the number of states that a computer can go through in the course of a computation will also be 2^s. The larger the number of storage cells in the machine the longer or more complex the sequence of states that it can go through.

To actually perform computation it is necessary to be able to modify the sequence of states that the computer goes through on the basis of input signals. To produce any useful effect the computer must generate one or more output signals, to indicate the result of the computation.

Consider a machine that has to recognize a 3 digit sequence and then respond with a yes or no according to whether or not the sequence was correct. An example might be digital door lock.

How should the state bits of a computer be organized?

1.1 STORE MODELS
There are 3 alternative models we can look at:

1. Each bit represents a state

2. Single state word

3. Random access store

1.1.1 Each Bit Represents a State
If each bit represents a state we could easily construct the door lock by stringing 4 cells together in sequence and having them activated sequentially by the logical AND of the signal from a button and the previous state. This is simple to implement and some digital logic used to be built this way, but it makes poor use of the state bits as we only get s rather than 2^s states.

1.1.2 Single State Word
This is in theoretical terms the ideal way to construct a computer. The state word is composed of the concatenation of all of the state cells. It can be treated as an s bit binary number. For large s the number of states possible becomes astronomical. A computer with a 64 bit status word could have a state to represent every centimeter of the distance between here and the nearest star. This sort of computer is a generalized finite state automaton . If the computer is organized as shown in Figure 1.2, then each bit of the present state can potentially influence any bit of the next state.

This architecture can go from any state to any other in a single cycle - from here to Alpha Centauri without stopping on the way. Each bit in the current state can be taken into account in determining the next state. All values of the input bits can be taken into account likewise. An implication of this is that each bit of the future state word depends upon each bit of the present state word. There must be wires provided to each state bit to logic that feeds each other state bit.

8   STORE BASED COMPUTATION [Ch.1

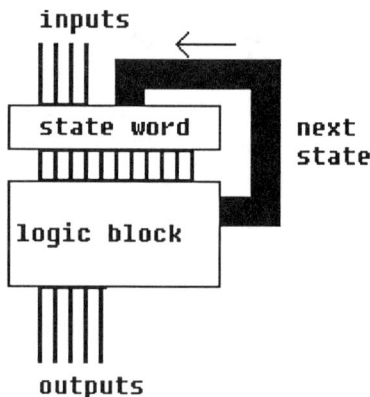

Figure 1.2 A generalized finite state automaton. Any bit in the state vector can influence the value of any other bit in the next time period.

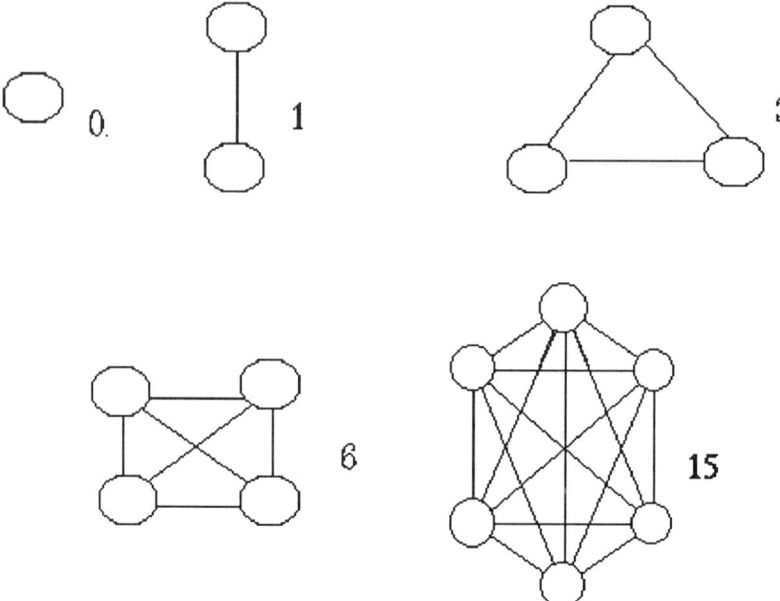

Figure 1.3 The wiring required for a generalized finite state automaton grows as the square of the number of state bits.

The drawback of this is the number of interconnection wires required to allow each state bit to affect the next state of every other bit, which goes up roughly as the square of the number of bits, and the number of logic cells (ANDs, ORs) to do this, which goes up as 2^s. This is illustrated in Figure 1.3. To be more precise: number of wires used to connect state cells in finite automata goes up as $s(s-1)$

1.1.3 Random Access Store

If instead of connecting all of the state cells to each other, we organise the state cells into many discrete words and lead these into a common logic block then we can diminish the number of wires considerably.

If we divide our s state bits into $w = s/b$ words each of b bits, and wire them up in a grid, we need only $(w+b)$ wires to join them to the common logic block. This is the random access memory computer. Like a generalized finite state automaton (FSA) it runs in a cycle. But it reads only part of the present state and modifies the state vector as a result of what it has read. It is less powerful than an FSA in that at most w bits of the state can be taken into account each cycle and at most w bits of the state altered in each cycle.

Machines built on the principles of RAS are either Von Neumann or Harvard machines. The Von Neumann machine has a single random access memory that can hold both instructions and data. The Harvard machines have two stores. The instructions are held in a Read Only Memory or ROM, and the data is held in a Read/Write Random Access Memory or RAM. Harvard machines are widely used for things like pocket calculators and washing machines. Larger computers tend to be based upon the Von Neumann model. The great bulk of modern computers fall into one or the other of these two classes.

In both Harvard and Von Neumann machines only a small subset of the computer's state bits can be changed each cycle. The limited rate at which the state vector can be changed with this wiring pattern is termed the Von Neumann bottleneck. It may be a considerable period before advances in connection techniques, perhaps using optical techniques, allow us to build machines that do not suffer from this limitation. Although there have been promising developments in the manufacture of parallel machines one finds that many of these are just collections of Von Neumann machines linked together. There is thus still considerable scope for computing paradigms that share with the Von Neumann machine a store that can only be modified a word at a time.

1.2 SECONDARY STORAGE AND TERMINATION.

A computer system is more than just a CPU and a random access memory. Nearly all computers have some form of secondary storage. Nowadays this will be in the form of disks, either hard disks or floppy disks. There is often a further layer of storage for archival purposes that uses magnetic tapes or optical disks. One of the less remarked upon aspects of the Von Neumann paradigm is that it ignores secondary storage.

When we are dealing with the Von Neumann architecture as an abstract model of computation we pretend that there is no such thing as disk storage. In the very earliest days of computers, this may have been justified but it is clearly an anachronism now. The fact that we persist with our oversight has, I think, something to do with the very notion of a computer. Computers originated in the 1940s. They arose from a combination of the researches of mathematicians into the basis of computability and the demands of physical scientists. Physicists wanted to do very hard sums the better to kill people. The biggest and most expensive computers are still devoted to hard sums and abstract discussion of the capabilities of computers is still mainly done by people with a mathematical training. As a result the idea that the function of computers is to perform computation tends to be taken for granted.

In practice, however, this is not what most computers are bought for. Most computers are sold for commercial data processing not computation. As data processing machines, their primary function is the storage and retrieval of information. They may perform calculations on the data they store, or have to perform calculations in order to store the data, but these are incidental. Academic computer scientists tend to look down their noses slightly at data-processing. It has the slightly unsavoury odour of trade. They like to think of their noble machines as being slightly above that. So they continue to call them computers rather than dators, business machines or as Jo Lyon called them: electronic offices.

From a computational point of view, the RAM of a computer is the only store that matters, and it only matters for the duration of the computation. We assume that the store is either undefined or cleared prior to the program starting. Once the program has terminated and output its answer,[9] then the state that the store is left in is of no concern.

The whole concept of a program which terminates, derives from a theory of computing machines. A program is something that you execute in order to find out an answer to a problem. If it does not terminate then you are in trouble. For an electronic office, on the other hand, termination is the last thing you want. Ideally you want a business machine that will run non-stop storing information infallibly, untiringly processing queries. From the business machine viewpoint the important part of a machine store is what it retains at the end of the day: the filestore. Remove half my RAM and I can still run jobs, if a bit slowly. Crash half my disks, burn my archive tapes and my business comes to a halt.

1.3 TWO CULTURES

Two cultures have arisen, one around data processing and one around computing. The data processing world has developed the database system. The computing world has developed the programming language. Obviously these two cultures are not totally independent. Data in databases is manipulated by programs written in programming languages so that interfaces have to exist between programming languages and database systems, but these interfaces have been of secondary concern both to mainstream programming language design and to database systems people. This is illustrated by the fact that each culture acknowledges only a very primitive form of the other.

Despite the recent spread of 4th generation languages, most existing database applications are written in COBOL, a very early programming language, which lacks many of the features now taken for granted in high level languages. On the other side of the divide most programming language designers have been even more conservative. They have relegated dealing with disk store to the category of input/output and provide little or no support for data storage. From the point of view of popular programming languages, disk store scarcely exists, let alone database management systems.

1.3.1 Thesis: disks as seen from programming languages

Pascal in its original specification it ignored disks completely.

> 'The human can submit his information via <u>input devices</u> (e.g. key punches, card readers, paper tapes, magnetic tapes, terminals) and receive his results via <u>output devices</u> (e.g. lineprinters, card and paper tape punches, terminals, visual display units.' (Pascal User Manual, K. Jensen and N.Wirth, Springer Verlag 1978)

Disk store disappears here into the general category of input output. Disks are not even mentioned. The representation of disk store within the language is as a sequential file. The characteristics of the sequential file are derived from the input output devices mentioned above: card readers, paper tape devices, magnetic tapes etc. Pascal's primitive operations on files only make sense in this context.

The program can perform the operations **get, put, reset, rewrite** on a file. Associated with the file **f** is a buffer variable designated **^f**. This buffer is treated as part of the normal random access store and can be assigned to in the usual way. On a **put** it is transferred to the file and on a **get** it is read from the file. Either of these operations advances the file by one data item. The names of the procedures **reset** and **rewrite** are revealing. They imply the notion of a tape that can be rewound back to its starting position. What is striking about these procedures is what they omit.

1.3.1.1 Absence of persistent names

A file variable may be declared in Pascal just like any other. You can place it in the global scope or in a local scope. In the one case it persists for the duration of the program, in the other it persists for the duration of the procedure in which it is called. This is consistent with the general scope rules of the language. The problem is that declaring a file variable does not allow you to do any operations on it other than assigning to or reading from its buffer variable. Unless you have first associated a file variable with an operating system file, you will get an input/output error reported if you attempt a **put** or a **get**. This is inconsistent with the rest of the language. If you declare an array you can start assigning to it immediately. Why should files be different?

1.3.1.2 Sequential access

Disks are random access devices. They may be rather slow compared to semiconductor memory but you can access any track without reading the intervening tracks. Pascal gives no hint of this. The **get** and **put** operations work in a strictly sequential manner. They force you to treat disks like magnetic tapes. The paradigm of input/output means that everything that is not RAM has to be coerced into the same model irrespective of its innate properties. The operations provided on disk files are thus the same as for teletypes, and the same as for VDUs. In all cases you perform sequential writes. This is inappropriate not only for disks but also for VDUs. By any rational conception a VDU is a two dimensional array of characters. It is only the intellectual conservatism of those who grew up with teletypes that presents it to us as a sequential device that scrolls upwards. Most operating systems now provide windowing packages that can be called to handle the screen, but the screen itself lacks linguistic representation. A consistent treatment of assignment in a language would extend it to include assignment to screen fields.

1.3.1.3 Lack of data type orthogonality

Pascal pretends to allow orthogonal input output. Seemingly you can write items of any data type to a file. Consider the program in Example 1.1

Writelist builds up a linked list of integers going from 100 down to 1 and writes the list out to a file of records. Since this example is in Turbo Pascal rather than ISO Standard Pascal a file assignment call is used to bind the file variable to an operating system file. This file is then read in by a second program shown in Example 1.2.

The program **readlist** reads in the records in the same order in which they were written out and then traverses the list writing out the values on the list. The result of executing it is undefined. This is because the pointers forming links between records are implemented as machine addresses. The values of these machine addresses are preserved in the file. When the records are read back in, the addresses into which they are read are likely to be different. This means that the **next** fields of the records point at the old machine addresses not the new ones. Traversing the list will probably lead into uninitialized areas of memory with unpredictable results.

This is a major inconsistency in the language because data-structures based upon records linked together with pointers are an important and frequently used attribute of Pascal. It means that for a whole class of data-structures there exists no ready means of long term storage. When one is producing a word processor one needs to use quite different data structures as soon as the the file is too big to fit into store.

Other leading programming languages do little better than Pascal.

Ada formalizes features that had become included as de facto standards in most Pascal implementations: a method of binding file variables to operating system files and a method of seeking to a position in a file. In Ada there are still major discrepancies in the way disk store is represented. Although programs can bind file variables to operating system files, the operating system files themselves remain outside the scope of the language. It also remains impossible to meaningfully transfer to disk any records that contain pointer variables.

At the level of formal definition the C language provides no operations on disks. All disk operations are done via external libraries of subroutines. These subroutines are standardized by convention to be the same as in the Unix implementations of C. They can be divided into two groups, those like **printf** concerned with formatted character transput and those that provide the low level unformatted data transput. The unformatted transput is provided directly by the Unix operating system primitives **read**, **write** and **seek**. These treat disk files as

```
program writelist(input,output);
type List = ^ ListElement;
    ListElement = record
                        next: List;
                        value: integer;
                  end;
    var f : file of ListElement;
        p,q : List;
        i : integer;


begin
    p := nil;
    for i:= 1 to 100 do
    begin
        new(q); q^.next:=p; q^.value:=i; p:=q;
    end;
    assign(f,'listfile');
    rewrite(f);
    while p <> nil do begin
        write(f,p^); p:=p^.next
    end;
end.
```
Example 1.1

unstructured arrays of bytes. Unlike arrays in programming languages disk files have a couple of special properties. One is that the default for subsequent accesses is sequential. If a program opens a disk file and **seeks** to position 100 and writes a byte then the next write will automatically go to location 101. A second property that follows on from this is that files are extensible. Programs can append characters to the end of a file. These properties of extensibility and sequential access are consequences of treating disk files, interprocess pipes and terminals in a fairly consistent way.

The facilities provided in C to access disks are a considerable improvement on what was available in Pascal. By treating files as a uniformly addressable array of bytes the programmer gets all the power of the Von Neumann store.

On this same foundation, the entire edifice of typing and advanced datastructures used in programming languages has been erected. The problem is that the disk is presented to the programmer in a completely raw form. It is like having a programming language in which the only type available was an array of characters. In some ways the situation is rather like that facing an assembly level programmer using an early 8 bit microprocessor.

On a chip like the z80 the store is a randomly accessed array of bytes, which must be handled a byte at a time. If assembly programmers wish to access any more complicated data structure, they have to do it by composing more primitive operations. If they want to access an array of records, they must do their own arithmetic to evaluate the base address of a given record, then add to it a field offset. It can be done. The wealth of software that was written in assembler for 8 bit micros is testimony to this. It does, however, take time and effort and is error prone. The same applies to trying to set up complicated data structures on disk in C.

With C there is still a problem if you want to save some kind of directed graph data-structure built up with pointers. The disk file under Unix is randomly accessible as is the RAM, but they are two different address spaces. The C language only supports pointer operations in one of these spaces: RAM.

1.3.2 Antithesis: the database view

The view of disks provided by programming languages is primitive compared to that evolved within the business machine community. The programming language designer is generally concerned with the problem of specifying algorithms to perform computation. The database systems designer is concerned with modelling the world in order to regulate some social process. The database systems designer concentrates on providing data modelling tools. If you are modelling some real system you do not want to be concerned with the properties of the storage device on which you keep the model. We find with DBMSs that the disk itself vanishes behind layers of abstraction. What the user is presented with is a modelling system, for instance relations, whose properties are defined at an abstract mathematical level. More or less incidentally, it is just taken as an obvious requirement that the system guarantee the physical integrity of the data and preserve it over long periods of time.

Tied in with a sophisticated and often very specialized system of data modelling a special purpose data manipulation language (DML) is provided. SQL is an example. These languages provide a mechanism for specifying queries over the stored data. In addition they may provide methods to update the

```
program readlist(input,output);
type List = ^ ListElement;

    ListElement = record
                    next: List;
                    value: integer;
                  end;
var f : file of ListElement;
    p,q : List;
    i : integer;


begin
    assign(f,'listfile');
    reset(f);
    new(p);
    read(f,p^);
    while not eof(f) do begin
        new(q); read(f,q^);
    end
    while p <> nil do begin
        writeln(output,p^.value);
        p:=p^.next;
    end;
end.
```
Example 1.2

database by inserting additional tuples into a relation or by deleting specified tuples from relations. These DMLs are tailored to the particular purpose of database query and update and lack some of the facilities that would now be considered essential in a programming language. General purpose programming languages invariably provide some mechanism for functional or procedural abstraction. They allow you to declare functions or procedures that encapsulate some sequence of operations that are either logically distinct or commonly used. It is also normal to provide some form of conditional operation, either in the form of **if then else**, or in the form of **case** statements. Data manipulation languages do not generally have these facilities. This restricts their usefulness in the specification of general purpose algorithms.

The type definition facilities of the database systems are richer than those of programming languages in some respects and poorer in others. They allow the usual set of base types as well as types like relations that are not generally supported by programming languages, but their provision for user defined types, enumerated types and pointer types is usually nil. The fields of tuples are specified in terms of pregiven base types.

It is implicit in the design of database systems that the data will be stored on disks. This means that data will hang around for a long time but the implementors must keep in mind the slower access time of disks. The need to minimize the number of disk accesses to perform an operation becomes a golden rule of the database system designer. This means that there is a preference in the DMLs for operations that transform large quantities of data. These enable data items that are adjacent to one another on disk to be brought into RAM in a single transfer. The lack of provision for procedures with local variables in data manipulation languages may be due to this emphasis on disk store. If procedures were allowed, and these could declare relations as local variables, and these relations had to be allocated on disk, then the cost of procedure calls would be considerable.

1.3.3 Synthesis: persistent programming

The strengths and weaknesses of database systems in comparison to general purpose algorithmic languages are summed up in Table 1.1.

It can be seen that in almost all respects the facilities provided by programming languages are equal or superior to those provided by database systems. The one shortfall is in the longevity of their data. The variables in programming languages exist for a period that varies from microseconds up to a few hours for a long running program. The data held by a DBMS is expected to last for years.

The objective of persistent programming is to implement programming languages in such a way that the longevity of their data can be extended over several years. This has to be done in a way that retains all of the facilities we have come to associate with modern high level languages. We must be able to write programs and procedures in the same way as before. We must be able to define all the same sorts of data-structures as before. The difference is that the data will now be able to persist for much longer. If this can be done, then both

	System DBMS	Programing Language
Base Types	strings numbers	strings numbers enumerated types
Type Constructors	relations records sets	arrays records sets pointers lists
Data Lifetime	years	seconds
Algorith Support	poor	extensive
Speed	slow	fast
Access Control	via schema	via scope rules or modules

Table 1.1

conventional filing systems and database management systems could be dispensed with. The argument goes that programming languages are sufficiently powerful to express all the properties of current databases. All they lack is the ability to apply their powerful data-structuring facilities to disk storage.

2

Origins and basics

2.1 ORIGINS OF PS-ALGOL
There are now a number of persistent programming languages. This book deals mainly with the language PS-algol. It was one of the first of the persistent programming languages to be designed and probably more effort has been put into its development than into most others.

PS-algol was created as the test of a hypothesis. The hypothesis was that merely by extending the longevity of its data, a high level programming language would be capable of replacing most of the functions of existing database systems. The hypothesis was advanced at the end of the 1970s by the research group in which I worked at Edinburgh University.

Th group was discontented with the slow and cumbersome nature of commercial database systems. They had found that the data models supported by commercial databases were unsuitable for tasks outside their immediate domain of application. Of particular concern was the area of computer aided design(CAD).

Large engineering projects require immense amounts of information to describe the object being designed. It is said that the weight of the documentation for an airliner is often greater than that of the plane itself. For many years large organizations have used computers to aid this design process. The computers have the job of storing the current state of the design and moving the design through successive versions as a result of the efforts of engineers.

The CAD problem has several aspects in common with keeping commercial records. The quantity of information is large: running into the gigabytes. The collection of data is very valuable. It represents the culmination of thousands of days of work and that is ultimately the reason why anything has value. Because organizations do not want to risk the loss of such precious data the method used to store it must be highly reliable.

The data collection is the product of collective work. Many people collaborate to produce a big design. Their work must be coordinated. Suppose several teams of designers are collaborating on a car design: an engine team, a body group, a suspension team etc. If a modification is made to the size of the engine, this information must be available to the body group. There must be some rules as to who can change a part of the design database so that the chassis people do not go in and change the diameter of the pistons.

At this level of generality much the same could be said of the requirements for a big financial database. Where database systems designed for commerce fall down in CAD is over their slowness and the inappropriateness of their data models. As an example let us look at the problem of a program that captures digital circuits by interacting with a designer via a graphics screen. It must capture the logical connectivity of the circuit and the aesthetic properties of the circuit schematic. In a language like Pascal it is possible to invent a set of data types that might serve.

First we must be able to represent components. A component has a type: it might be an 80386 microprocessor for example. It has a position on the drawing and a position on the circuit board. It has an orientation on the drawing: vertical, horizontal, mirror imaged. It will have a part number and a set of wires connecting it to other components. A possible declaration of the type component might be:

```
type
 component = record
       whatsort: chiptype;
       drawing,board: position;
       orientation: (vertical,horizontal);
       mirrored : boolean;
```

                PartNo : **string**[6];
                wires : ^ pinlist;
end;

        position =   **record**
                x,y: integer;
        end

The types of chip like a 80386 will themselves need a data-structure to describe them. They will be made up of a collection of pins, a partname, a manufacturer etc:

        type
                chiptype = ^ chip;
                chip = **record**
                        partname, manufacturer : string[20];
                        packagetype :(DIP, PGA, LCC , SIP);
                        Pincount   : **integer;**
                        pins : ^connections;
                end;
                connections = **record**
                        next : ^ connections;
                        pinnumber : string[4];
                        sort: (inputpin, outputpin, power,
                                        ground, bidirectional);
                        signalname: string[8];
                        positionOnDiagram: **record**
                                side: (left, right);
                                positionfromtop:**integer;**
                        end;
                end;

These data types are enough to describe the chips and their layout on the diagram. To link them up CAD systems use the concept of a net. A net is a group of points that are electrically connected. We need to be able to get from a chip to the set of nets to which it is connected. This might be done using the type pinlist:

```
pinlist = record
        wire : ^ net;
        pin  : ^ connections;
        next : ^ pinlist;
end
```

A net itself would have a name, a list of things that it was connected to and a list of points on the drawing through which the wire passed.

```
net =   record
          netname:string[20];
          attachments: ^link;
          Anchors: ^drawingpnts;
end;

link =  record
          next: ^link;
          chip: ^component;
          pin: ^connections;
end;

drawingpnts = record
          next: ^drawingpnts;
          where: position;
end;
```

The overall effect of these types is shown in Figure 2.1. Just to describe a relatively simple sort of design, a circuit schematic, has involved us in declaring a lot of types. In a real example the number of types needed would have been greater because no account has been taken of things like capacitors, resistors etc. Obviously if we wanted to model a three dimensional structure rather than an simple flat drawing the set of types would be even more complicated. The example up to now has been given in Pascal. Consider the difficulties of translating this into a relational database.

It was because neither conventional programming languages nor conventional database systems were suited to the problem of CAD data storage that PS-algol was developed. The hypothesis on which it was built was that the only extra feature that a modern programming language needed to have to be suitable for data intensive work was the addition of persistent memory. It was assumed that all of the data structuring primitives required were already present in existing programming languages and were already used for transitory information storage. If these features could be extended to cover data stored on the disk in a transparent fashion then it would be unnecessary to use complex database packages.

The fact that PS-algol was developed rather than a Persistent Pascal, for instance, was a matter of expediency. Pascal compilers are large and the Edinburgh group did not fancy having to make changes to such a large piece of software. The same applied to Algol68 which was another suitable candidate for

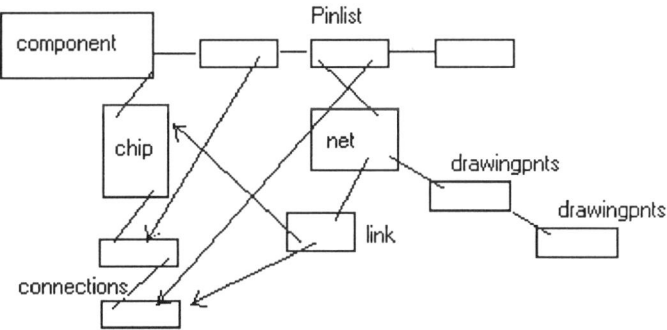

Figure 2.1

persistence. Instead we chose to develop a language called S-algol. S-algol had been invented at St Andrews University by Ron Morrison as part of his PhD research. Its compiler is very short, about 2000 lines, and easy to understand. In fact in order to decide which language to work with the group put compiler listings of the Algol68C compiler, the Wirth Pascal compiler and the S-algol compiler next to one another on a shelf and chose the one with the thinnest listing.

The early releases of PS-algol were syntactically identical to the original S-algol. The only changes made were the addition of a few extra library procedures to control the persistent store. It was necessary to make a few changes to the binary code that was generated and to the run time system but these were invisible to the PS-algol programmer. At this stage it was possible to take any

S-algol program and run it straight away on the PS-algol system.

At a later stage a number of extensions were made to the type system of the language and PS-algol began to diverge from S-algol. In this book the syntax presented will be that of the 1985 release of the PS-algol reference manual. Where necessary it will be explained how other versions of the language differ from this release. In the section on implementation structure, more details will be given of earlier and later releases: the process of evolution of the run time system helps understanding of the problems that must be faced when implementing a persistent programming language.

2.2 BASICS
2.2.1 Base types
The base types provided by the PS-algol language are booleans, integers, reals and strings. Each of the base types has a literal representation: they can be written down using the character set of the language. This literal representation may of course be quite different from the representation of the types in persistent memory.

2.2.1.1 Bool
The boolean type is a set with two elements that are denoted by the literal values **true, false**. Within PS-algol the boolean type is referred to by the abbreviation **bool**.

2.2.1.1 Int
The integer type is the set of whole numbers. On a given machine only a subset of the whole numbers will actually be available since the internal representation of the integers is in a fixed length machine word. Only positive integers have literal representations:

<int-literal> ::= [0-9]* | **maxint**

That is to say a positive integer is denoted either by a sequence of one or more decimal digits or by the word **maxint** which denotes the largest integer the implementation can handle. The abbreviation **int** is used in the language to refer to values that belong to the set of integers.

Examples of integer literals are:

1   2   24   987   0000

2.2.1.3 Real

The type **real** in the PS-algol language is used to describe the set of values that can be represented using 64 bit floating point numbers within a computer memory. These are approximations to the mathematician's concept of a real number.

The literal notation for them is:

<real-literal>::=

<int.literal>.[<int.literal>][e[+l-]<int-literal>]|
<int.literal>[e[+l-]<int-literal>]|maxreal|pi|epsilon

In the above grammar notation [] means that the production is optional. Examples of real literals are:
   1.5
   1.
   1e6
   176.6e-9

In this notation the [e[+l-]<int-literal>] part denotes the power of ten by which the preceding number is to be multiplied to obtain the value of the literal.

2.2.1.4 String

A **string** literal is written down as a sequence of characters enclosed in quotes thus:

    """"   ! a string with no characters in it
    "**this is a string**"   ! this on the other hand is a comment
    "**The string can be up to 65535 characters long. Unlike some other languages PS-algol allows strings to extend over several lines of text. This allows a whole paragraph to be formatted as a single string.**"

It is sometimes useful to have special characters included in a string. Characters like backspace or carriage return are difficult to enter into a literal using a conventional text editor so that provision is made to represent them by using escape sequences that start with a single quote.
       '**n**   means new line
       ''   means '

```
''' means ''
't  means tab
'p  means new page
'o  means carriage return
'b  means backspace
```

2.2.2 Expressions

Expressions provide a means of constructing new values from existing ones. Each expression has a value which is the result of evaluating it. The value will belong to one of the types of the language. This is then said to be the type of the expression. Thus we can have integer expressions, real expressions etc.

```
    1
```
is an integer literal
```
    1+3
```
is an integer expression. The character + is termed a dyadic operator: it takes two integers and returns a third. PS-algol expressions are composed of a combination of operators and the round brackets characters (and). Some of these operators are the familiar dyadic ones. Others are monadic: ones that take only a single value as input. Yet others are polyadic operators which take 3, 4, 5 or more arguments as inputs. As a result expressions in PS-algol can be very complex compared to those in a language like Pascal.

The function of the ()s in expressions is to determine the order of evaluation of sub-expressions within an expression. They force all of the values and operators within the () to be evaluated first. Otherwise the order of evaluation is determined by the priority of the operators which specify for example that:
```
    4+5*7
```
is equivalent to
```
    4+(5*7)
```
but not equivalent to
```
    (4+5)*7
```

2.2.2.1 Monadic Operators

There are two monadic operators - and ~. The operator -, pronounced "minus", converts a real or integer number into its negative. The operator ~, pronounced "not" negates the value of a boolean expression. It maps **true** to **false** and vice versa. The monadic operators are highest in priority.

2.2.2.2 Dyadic Operators

There are fifteen dyadic operators on the base types plus several more on the advanced types.

There are two operators that work on all types, = and ~= pronounced "equal to" and "not equal to". Their two operands must be both of the same type and the result of evaluating the expression is a boolean value indicating whether or not the operands were equal to one another.

    3 = 5   -> **false**
    (2+3) = 5   -> **true**

In the above example, and in others the arrow -> indicates the result of evaluating an expression. The arrow and the result are not part of the PS-algol, they are put in for explanation. The types integer, real and string are ordered. If you have two values from one of these types the values are either equal to one another or one is less than the other. There is a set of operators that test these relationships < <= > >= pronounced "less than", "less than or equal to", "greater than", "greater than or equal to". In the case of integers the semantics of these operators are obvious.

In the case of real numbers the semantics of the operators are determined by the floating point hardware of the machine the language runs upon. It should be recognised that spurious results can be obtained due to the finite approximation to real numbers that are used. If the difference between two real numbers is less than the predefined real literal **epsilon** then they will appear to be equal.

For strings the ordering relationship is based upon the ordering of the characters of the string in the ASCII. The ordering rule for strings requires the notion of a substring. In PS-algol a substring can be extracted from a string as follows:

    "Janus" (3 | 2)   -> "nu"

    "Janus" (1 | 3)   -> "Jan"

    "Janus" (2 | 4)   -> "anus"

    "Janus" (1 | 12)   -> this gives an error and halts

    1. Two strings are equal if they contain the same characters in the same order.

    2. String A is less than string B if the length of string A is N and the length of B is greater than N and the substring formed from the first N characters

of B is equal to A.

3. String A is less than string B if for some N in the range zero to the length of string A - 1, A(1|N) = B(1|N) and A(N|1)<B(N|1).

The comparison operators evaluate to a boolean. More complex boolean expressions can be constructed using the operators **and** and **or**. They follow the normal boolean semantics for and/or. These are not simply logical operators, they also affect the order of evaluation of sub-expressions. In the expression:

    1 < 2 **or** 4 >= 3   -> **true**

the computer will only evaluate the sub-expression (1 < 2). This returns true which makes it unnecessary to evaluate the second part (4 >= 3). Similarly in the expression:

    1 > 2 **and** 4 >= 3   -> **false**

only the sub-expression (1 > 2) is evaluated since this makes it unnecessary to evaluate the second sub-expression.

The operators **+ - *** pronounced as "plus", "minus", "times" perform addition subtraction and multiplication on arbitrary mixtures of integer and real numbers. If any component of the expression is a real then the result will be a real rather than an integer. Division is treated differently. The operator **/** takes two numbers of either type and evaluates to a real number. For integers there are two additional operators :

    div takes two integer operands and returns the result of division rounded down to an integer.

    7 **div** 3   -> 2

    rem returns the remainder after integer division.

    11 **rem** 3   -> 2

Strings can be concatenated using the operator ++.

    "Janus" ++ "the god"   -> "Janusthe god"

In PS-algol the priorities of the operators are as shown:

High

()

:=

* / div rem ++

+ -

 is isnt < > >= <= ~= =

and

or

Low

There are other dyadic operators that work on pictures and pixels but these will be dealt with in the appropriate place.

2.2.2.3 Triadic operators

We have already presented one triadic operation : substring extraction. This takes as operands a string and two integers. There are several triadic operations on pictures, but the other basic triadic operation is selection. This is performed by a triadic operator **if A then B else C**. In this the expression **A** must be of type boolean and the expressions **B** and **C** may be of any type provide both are of the same type. For example:

    if 1<4 **then** "one" **else** "four"   ->"one"
    if false then maxint **else** 0   -> 0

The notion of a selection expression may seem unusual if you are used to the Pascal style of programming but it is standard in Algol-like languages.

2.2.2.4 Polyadic operations

There are several polyadic operations that produce a single value from 4 or more input values. Most of these are specialized and will be dealt with under the heading of the graphical types. There is one polyadic operator of general significance which is a generalization of the selection operation. Examples of this are:

    case 17654 **rem** 3 **of**
    1,2 : "not a multiple"
    default: "a multiple"   -> "not a multiple"

    case true of
        "janus"(1|3) ="nus" : 1
        pi = 22/7, pi = 3   : 2
        659*8 =5272 : 2+1
    default   : 0   -> 3

What happens with this is that the expression between the **case** and the **of** is evaluated. It is then matched in sequence against the values derived from evaluating the subsequent <NONVOID-clauses> and if there is a match it returns the value derived from evaluating the expression following the colon. If no match is found then the default value is returned.

2.2.3 Identifiers

Identifiers are names which may be attached to values or to storage locations containing values. This is a slightly different approach from that taken in most imperative languages where identifiers are the names of storage locations. It is also different from that of applicative languages where identifiers are just names for values. An identifier is introduced by means of the word **let**.

    let a = 7
    let a.over.pi = a / pi
    let jupiter = "Zeus"
    let yes = **true**

In the above we have made certain identifiers identical to the values on the right. The string "Zeus" and the identifier **jupiter** may now be substituted for one another lower down in the program without changing its meaning. These identifiers are typed as follows:

identifier	type
a	**cint**
a.over.pi	**creal**
jupiter	**cstring**
yes	**cbool**

These are all identifiers for constants. The value of the identifier cannot change during the program. This, and indeed everything presented so far, is part of the functional subset of the language in which referential transparency is preserved. The phrase referential transparency means that a given expression yields the same value at all times. This is only true because we have not yet introduced the assignment operation.

Note that the full stop character is a valid part of an identifier and that upper and lower case identifiers are distinct.

Referential transparency breaks down when we introduce the store. This is done by identifying locations in the store. For example:

    let i:= 1

declares **i** to be a location in the store that will always contain an integer and whose initial value is to be 1. Because the declaration is associated with initialization, there can never be any uninitialized variables in PS-algol. The type of the store location is deduced by the compiler from the initial value.

2.2.4 Statements
The introduction of the store allows assignment statements which update store locations.

    let i:= 4
    let j = 2
    i:= i **div** j

The value of **i** is changed as a result of the assignment statement from 4 to 2. A store location has either its initial value or the value that was last assigned to it. Hence the following program fragment will write "true true"

    let a:=b
    write a = b
    a:=c
    write a = c

With the existence of store it is possible to construct programs with bounded loops. PS-algol provides two looping mechanisms: the for loop and the while loop.

    let square = **read.r**()
    let root := 1.0
    let diff:=1.0
    while (diff*diff)>epsilon **do** {

        diff := square -(root*root);
        root := root + diff/ (2*root)

    }
    write "square root of ",square," is ",root

Here we see the input output primitives **read.r** which reads a real number from the keyboard, and **write** which writes a list of values to the screen. The while loop goes on repeating so long as the test condition holds. In the course of the loop the identifier root takes on a succession of values. Note that curly brackets { } can be used to group statements into a block that is treated as a single compound statement.

To handle the case where the terminating condition comes at the end of the loop the **repeat .... while** construct should be used.

```
let square = read.r()
let root := 1.0
let diff:=1.0
repeat
        diff := square -(root*root);
        root := root + diff/ (2*root)
while (diff*diff)>epsilon
write "square root of ",square," is ",root
```

For loops whose number of repetitions is known prior to entry into the loop the **for** statement is provided.

```
for square = 10 to 100 by 10 do {
   let root := 1.0
   let diff:=1.0
   repeat
        diff := square -(root*root);
        root := root + diff/ (2*root)
   while (diff*diff)>epsilon
   write "square root of ",square," is ",root
}
```

In the case of the for loop the loop variable (square in the example) is implicitly declared as a cint. This ensures that the loop terminating condition can not be tampered with by code inside the loop. The starting value, the terminating value and the loop step are all evaluated once at the start of the loop.

2.2.5 Blocks

A block is delimited either by a { ... } pair or a **begin .. .end** pair. The scope of an identifier is from the statement following its declaration to the end of the block. The usual Algol scope rules apply. As will be seen these have some interesting implications when combined with first class functions and a persistent store.

A block can return a value. The value of a block is the value of the last expression in the block.

2.2.6 Procedures
Procedures in PS-algol are values. They are identified like any other value, using a **let** statement.

```
let sqrt = proc( real square ->real)
    {
        ! everything in the brackets is the procedure body
        let root := 1.0
        let diff:=1.0
        repeat
            diff := square -(root*root)
            root := root + diff/ (2*root)
        while (diff*diff)>epsilon
        ! the next line is the  result
        root
    }
```

In the above example the identifier sqrt is bound to the procedure literal on the right hand side of the equals sign. A procedure literal is made up of a type specification followed by a clause. The type specification performs three functions:

1. It identifies the types of the parameters that must be passed in when the procedure is called.
2. It identifies the type of the result returned.
3. It assigns local identifiers to the parameters.
    A procedure is called in the usual way:
sqrt(4)   -> 2.0

Parameters are passed by value. Although it is possible within the body of a procedure to assign to parameters, this only affects the parameter itself. Thus:

```
{
        let dummy = proc( int a.copy)
            begin
                a.copy :=9
            end
        let four := 4
        dummy(four)
        sqrt(four)
}
        -> 2.0
```

In this example the value associated with four is not altered by the assignment statement in the procedure dummy. The only way by which a procedure can communicate with its calling environment is by returning a result. This makes PS-algol have a rather functional feel to it.

The original S-algol syntax for procedures was slightly different. In S-algol procedures were not first class citizens. It was not possible to have procedure variables. An example of the old syntax for a procedure is:

```
procedure max(int a,b ->int)
begin
        if a>b then a else b
end
```

This syntax was retained on the first version of PS-algol under Vax VMS and for the IBM PC version. As will be explained later, procedures specified in this way can be implemented more efficiently.

3

Maps

A map associates elements of one set with elements of another. The mapping operation is one of the most fundamental operations in programming. In most programming languages this one operation appears in a number of different guises. In PS-algol all forms of map have the same syntax. We write mapping operation thus: **M(e)**. What it means is illustrated by Figure 3.1.

The map **M** when *applied* to an element of set1 **e**, returns an element of set2 designated **M(e)**. Maps in PS-algol come in two forms: algorithmic maps and storage maps.

We have already come across one form of map: the procedure. Procedures are algorithmic maps.

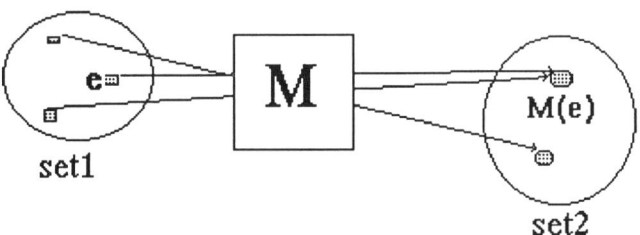

Figure 3.1 The idea of a map

36 MAPS [Ch.3]

The procedure sqr shown below maps from the set of integers to the set of squares of integers.

let sqr = **proc**(**int** an.integer -> **int**)
begin
an.integer * an.integer
end

It does this by providing an algorithm by which the square of an integer is to be computed. In this case the algorithm is simple:

To obtain the square of an integer:
"take an integer and multiply it by itself, the result is the sqr of the integer"

Using this algorithm we can obtain the area of squares with integral sides. The procedure sets up a mapping between the straight lines of integral length and the squares derived from them. This is shown conceptually in Figure 3.2.

This is a very simple algorithmic map. The sets between which the map operates are easily understood. When we write down a procedure we specify, at least partially, what these sets are. We show the mapping by means of an arrow going from the parameters of the procedure to the result. This mapping is the type of the procedure. The type of sqr is (**int** -> **int**).

This mapping is *total*. With every integer it associates a square. Consider the sqrt procedure given in the last chapter. This associated squares of real

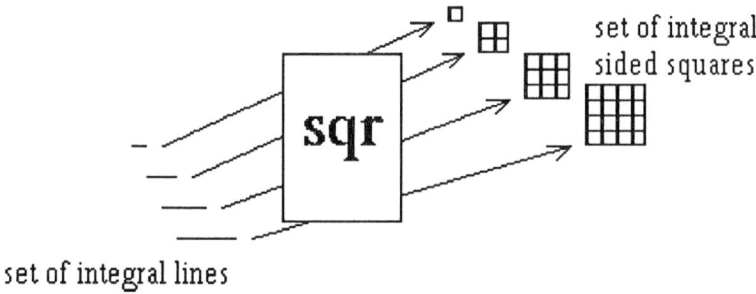

Figure 3.2 The mapping from lines to

valued area with their sides.
let sqrt = **proc(real** square **->real)**
{
    let root := 1.0
    let diff:=1.0
    repeat
        diff := square -(root*root)
        root := root + diff/ (2*root)
    while (diff*diff)>epsilon
    root
}

The mapping here is not fully specified by the procedure's type. The type is just (**real -> real**). But not all real values correspond to the areas of squares. The number -1.0 is a real value, but there is no square with this area. If we try to map the number -1.0 with sqrt what will happen?

The variables root and diff will take on this sequence of values

root	diff
1.0	
1.0	1.0
1.0	-2.0
0.0	-2.0
0.0	-1.0

The program terminates with an error trying to evaluate (0.0 -1.0/(0.0)).

This error occurs because the square root function is a partial map from the real numbers to the real numbers. It fails to map the negative real numbers because the concept of a negative area is undefined. This shows us some important things about maps. Maps can be *partial*. A partial map may only be successfully applied to a subset of its parameter type. A partial algorithmic map may fail for two reasons. It may go into an infinite loop, or it may attempt to perform an illegal operation. In the case we have just looked at the illegal operation was division by zero. If we look at this more closely, we see that the reason division by zero leads to failure is that division is itself a partial map of form (**real,real ->real**). The division map is undefined for division by zero.

The computer hardware works by implementing a small number of primitive maps, typically including the binary arithmetic and logical operations. The hardware detects when it is asked to perform a primitive map which is undefined. When this occurs it stops the program.

This concept of partiality is important in understanding the storage maps

38 MAPS [Ch.3

provided by PS-algol.

When talking about division we said that it was a mapping of type (**real,real ->real**). We can think of it as going from points in two dimensional Cartesian space onto the real number line. A similar characterization can be given to the other arithmetic operators.

Here the elements of the set that are being mapped are not simple numbers, but pairs of numbers. The division operator goes from a subset of the set (**real,real**) to the set **real**.

The set (**real,real**) corresponds to the Cartesian plane. By extension any space defined by an ordered sequence of types is a Cartesian product space. The procedures of PS-algol constitute maps from the set of Cartesian product spaces characterized by the types of their parameters. Those that return no result can be considered maps onto the empty set.

3.1 VECTORS
Cartesian product spaces can be made up of any ordered sequence of types. We can define procedures over any of these. In programming you frequently define procedures with different types of parameters. One might define the procedure

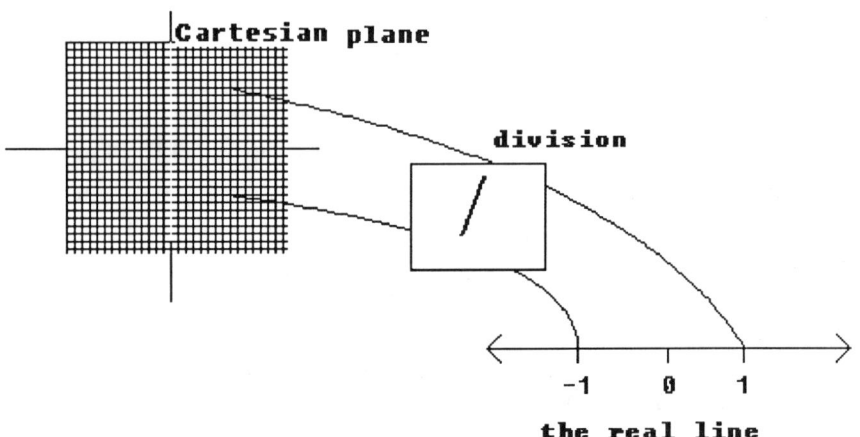

Figure 3.3 The division operator is a partial map from the cartesian plane to the real line.

procedure substr.of.length.starting.with(
    string s1;
    int l;
    string s2 ->**string**)

to find the substring s2 of length l in string s1. In this case the Cartesian product space is of mixed type.

The classical type of Cartesian product is however the vector. A simple vector is shown in Figure 3.4.

A vector of 2 integers defines a point on a grid. A vector of 2 reals defines a point in continuous 2 dimensional Cartesian space. A vector like [0.1,1.0,1.2] defines a point in continuous 3 dimensional Cartesian space. PS-algol allows you to write down vectors which define points in spaces of arbitrary dimension. If you wish you may write down a vector that defines a point in 8, 10 or 100 dimensional space. If we define a point in **n** dimensional space by the vector

$$[e_1, e_2, e_3, ..., e_n]$$

Then the values e_i separated by commas are termed the elements of the vector. If these are real numbers, then e_i specifies the projection of the point onto the ith axis of the **n** dimensional space. In the vector [3,2] the first element is conventionally taken to represent the projection of the point onto the horizontal axis. In this case it specifies that the point is 3 units along from the origin. This projection operation is itself a mapping of the integers onto the elements of the vector. Because projection is a mapping we can write it down the same way the application of procedures.

If **v** is a vector then the effect of projecting the vector along its ith dimension is written **v(i)**. Applying the vector as a map to the integers yields an element of the vector. We still need however a defined convention for numbering of elements. We could just say that the elements of a vector would always be numbered from 1 to n. But this is not always convenient. It is better if you can renumber the elements of a vector. Consider the following example:

    let uk.psbr = @ 1982 **of creal** [
        4.954e+9, 1.162e+10, 1.021e+10, 7.641e+9
    ]

This line of PS-algol defines the British public sector borrowing requirement in £ sterling from 1982 to 1985. Here the vector defines a point in 4 dimensional space, but we have labeled the dimensions to correspond to years. The public sector borrowing requirement for 1985 would be expressed:

    uk.psbr (1985)

Up to now all the examples of vectors have been numeric. But you can

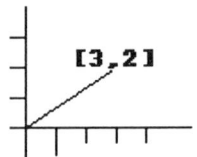

Figure 3.4 The vector [3,2]

have vectors of other types as well:
    let v2 = **@2 of cstring**["two", "three", "four"]

With this sort of thing we move into the realm of very abstract vector spaces to which it is difficult to give a geometric interpretation. We can still draw a picture though: Figure 3.5.

3.1.1 Constancy of Vectors

Like all **let** declarations, the declaration of a vector is made up of a left hand side and a right hand side. The left hand side contributes an identifier and the right hand side a value. If the declaration uses an = it acts to identify the value. In the previous example v2 *is* the name of **@2 of cstring**["two", "three", "four"].

If the declaration uses a := then the identifier becomes the name of a storage location that *holds* the value.
    let v3 := **@1 of cstring** ["one", "two", "three"]
means "create a store location, put the point in vector space described by **@1 of cstring** ["one","two","three"] into that location, then name the location v3" Since v3 is a location in store, it can hold another value:
    v3:= **@1 of cstring** ["ich", "ni", "san"]

Assignment of a vector is conceptually the same as any other assignment. It is no different from assigning a string or real. Certain obvious consequences follow from assignment of a vector. We know that the following program fragment must print "true":
    a:=b
    write a = b
from the definition of assignment. Hence by extension to the vectors declared previously
    v3:=v2

write v3 = v2

will also print "true". By extension if v3 = v2 then v3(i) = v2(i) for all i over which v3(i) is defined. In other words if two vectors are the same, the effect of projecting them along their axes is the same.

In geometry the elements of a vector are values. In a computer the elements of a vector can be storage locations whose value varies over time. In our declarations above, we have specified the vector as being made up of constant strings. Suppose we made the following declaration

let numerals =@1 **of string** ["I", "II", "III", "IV", "V"]

then the following program fragment would print out "IIV"

write numerals(1),numerals(4)

But since the elements of numerals are declared to be **string** rather than **cstring** they designate updateable store locations rather than values. So we can update the projections of the vector:

numerals(3) := "iii"

write numerals(3),numerals(4)
            -> "iiiIV"

We know that if v3 = v2 then v3(i) = v2(i) so it follows that

let romans =@1 **of string** ["I", "II", "III", "IV", "V"]

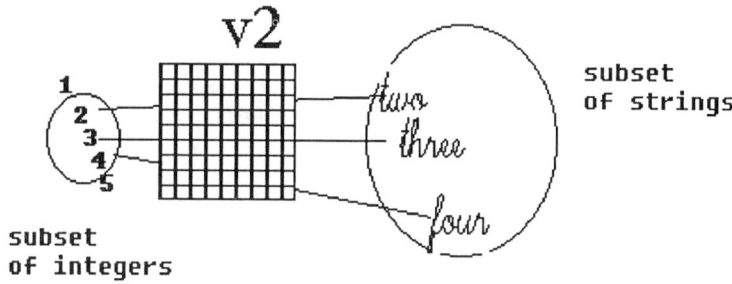

Figure 3.5 Projecting a vector along its dimensions

let arabs =@ 1 of string ["1", "2", "3", "4"]
let numerals := romans
write numerals(4)
romans(4) := "IIII"
write numerals(4)
numerals:=arabs
write numerals(4)
-> "IVIIII4"

If **v** is a vector then it will be composed of consecutively numbered elements. The numbers applied to the elements are termed indices. The highest index to which the vector can be applied is termed its upper bound. The lowest index is its lower bound. In the S-algol family of languages these are written **upb** and **lwb**. These are maps of the form (**vector -> int**).

The type of a vector may be written as the type of its elements prefixed by a *. A vector of integers has type *int. A vector of strings has type *string. The vector of *int

let Pascal = @1 of *int [
              @1 of int [1],
              @1 of int [1, 1]
              @1 of int [1, 2, 1]
              @1 of int [1, 3, 3, 1]]

has type **int .

A further method of creating updateable vectors is provided:
let v4 := vector a::b of 0
let v5 := vector x::y ,a::b of r

v4 is of type *int . v5 is of type **int. a,b,x, y,r are of type int.

This form is useful when the size of the vector that will be needed is not known at compile time. At run time the variables a,b,x,y are assigned values prior to the creation of the vector. All of the elements of the vector are initialized to the same value, 0 in the case of v4 and r in the case of v5.

A vector of type **t is a map from a subset of the Cartesian product space (**int, int**) onto **t**. Thus type **t may be thought of as equivalent to (**int,int->t**). In particular a **cint may be used in the same way as a procedure of type (**int,int -> int**). In the expression

P(1, 3) **div** 2

P could be either a procedure or a vector. As a matter of programming practice, it is often more efficient to use a vector as a look up table instead of a procedure to perform a mapping operation. The substitution of storage maps for algorithmic maps is a powerful optimization technique in programming.

Vectors of type **t are sometimes loosely called 2 dimensional vectors. This terminology is potentially confusing since the *real denoted by

@1 **of** real[0.1,9.2]

can take on values of its elements which define a continuous 2 dimensional vector space. When people call a **int a 2 dimensional vector they are describing the dimension of the Cartesian product space of the vector's indices rather than the space of the vector itself, which may well have many more than 2 dimensions.

Another way of looking at a **t is as a (**int** -> (**int->int**)). Thus

let pas2: = Pascal(2)

declares pas2 to be a *int, and

write Pascal(3) (2)

-> 2

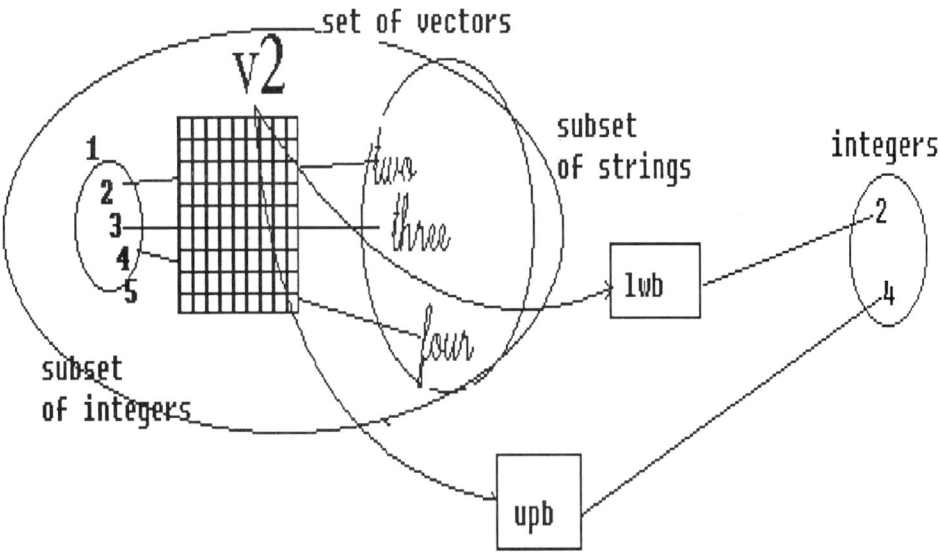

Figure 3.6 Predefined maps on the vectors

3.2 PNTRS

The **pntr** type, pronounced pointer, is a partial storage map from identifiers to values. If **p** is a **pntr** and **x** is an identifier then **p(x)** is the value obtained by applying the pointer to the identifier. Because **pntrs** are partial maps they are only defined for certain identifiers. You can not take an arbitrary pointer and an arbitrary identifier and apply the pointer to the identifier. The set of identifiers for which a pointer is defined form what is termed the class of that pointer. Classes are ordered finite sets of identifiers. They are defined as shown in the following example.

>   **structure** person(
>   **int** year.of.birth;
>   **string** forename,surname
>   )

This defines a class of identifiers { year.of.birth, forename, surname }. Associated with each identifier in the class is a type. Once such a class has been defined, pointers may be created that map from these identifiers to values.
   let p = person(1987, ''Mathew'', ''Lavell'')
This defines p to be a map from the set of identifiers defined by the class of persons to a set of associated values (see Figure 3.7). The maps are potentially updateable. In the above example we could alter the mapping performed by p as follows:
   p(forename):= ''Fiona''

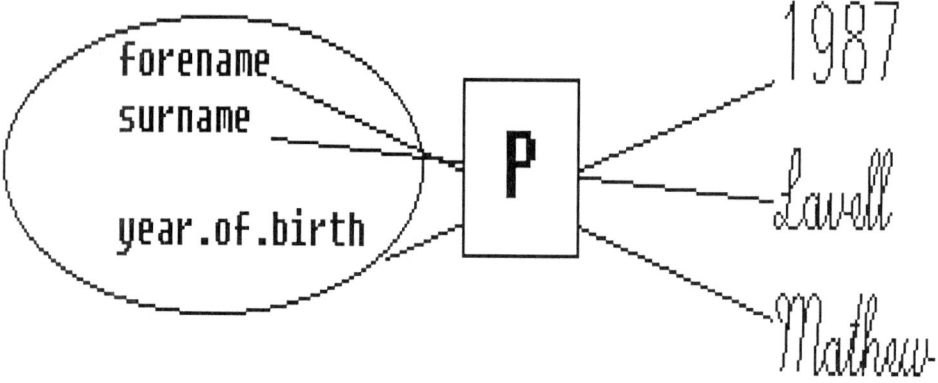

Figure 3.7 The idea of a **pntr**

If the identifier forename had been declared to be a string constant as in
structure person(**cint** year.of.birth; **cstring** forename,surname)
then the mapping from forename to strings effected by **p** would not be updateable.

Which set of identifiers are mapped by a pointer can be determined by use of the is operator. If **p** is a pointer and **c** a class of identifiers, then

p is c

eg:- x **is** person

is a boolean expression that takes on the value true if **p** maps the identifiers in c.

There exists a pointer that maps the empty set of identifiers. This pointer is called **nil**. There exists a predefined mapping called *class.identifier* that maps pointers to strings. This can be used at run time to discover what class a pointer belongs to.

3.3 TABLES

Tables are to strings what vectors are to integers. Just as vectors are maps from the integers to a type, tables are maps from strings to a type. They were introduced with a procedural interface originally, and given syntactic support in the IBM PC/AT release.

The syntax for a table literal value is shown in the following example.
tab cint of
''Hastings'':1066
''Culloden'':1745
''Stalingrad'':1942
default: 0

This table value is shown in Figure 3.8. As usual we can name the value:
let dateof = **tab cint of**
''Hastings'':1066
''Culloden'':1745
''Stalingrad'':1942
default: 0

We can apply the map to a string and get an integer back:

let battle = read.a.line()
write ''the year of '',battle,'' was '',dateof(battle)

>Culloden
                -> the year of Culloden was 1745
>Bannockburn
                -> the year of Bannockburn was 0

Tables (provided that they are not constant ones like the above) may be updated by assignment like other storage maps.
    structure address(**cstring** street,city)
    let people := **tab pntr of**
        default : nil
    people(''P Cockshott''):= address(''Richmond St'',''Glasgow'')

In the above example, an empty map from strings to pntrs is created. At first this returns nil whatever it is applied to. Next it is updated to map my name to my address. From then on it will return my address when applied to my name. The type of people would be written $pntr. The $ is used the same way for tables as * is for vectors, so you can have tables of tables as in $$**int**.

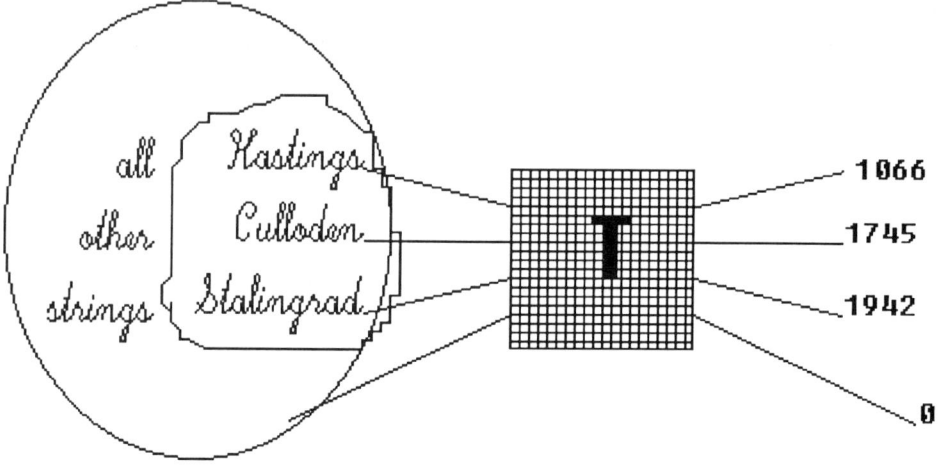

Figure 3.8 The idea of a table

4

Graphics types

In the last chapter we talked about how a 2 element vector like [x, y] defines a point in a Cartesian product space. If the types of x and y are **real** then that space is the familiar continuous 2 dimensional space of plane geometry. PS-algol recognizes vectors of this type as a special case.

    let point = [1.0, 2.3]

Is a valid declaration in PS-algol. It defines point to be of type **pic** which is short for picture. A point is the simplest picture that you can define. A picture is treated as an ordered non-empty set of points. In other words a picture is a collection of points joined by lines. There are two binary operators defined on pictures: join and combine. These operate between the last point of the first picture and the first point of the last picture(Figures 4.1-4.3).

Figure 4.1 let p1 = [1.0,1.0]   **Figure 4.2 let** p2 = [2.0,2.0]

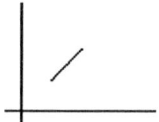

Figure 4.3 let l45 = p1 ^ p2

4.1 JOIN AND COMBINE

Join, written ^ , takes two pictures and joins them with a line.

With it we can define a procedure to make a square with bottom left corner [x,y] and side d as follows

> **let** square = **proc** (**real** x,y d->**pic**)
> **begin**
> > **let** origin = [x,y]
> > origin ^ [x,y+d] ^[x+d,y+d] ^ [x+d,y] ^ origin
>
> **end**

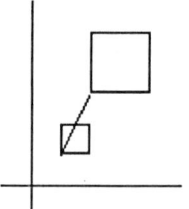

Figure 4.4 square(1.0,1.0,1.0) ^ square(2.0,3.0,2.0)

Such squares can be joined with lines as shown in Figure 4.4.

Using the combine operator &, pictures can be combined without joining lines.

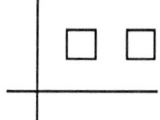

Figure 4.5 square(1,0,1.0,1.0) & square(3.0,1.0,1.0)

4.2 TRANSFORMATIONS

There are operators that perform the basic geometric transformations on pictures. A picture can be scaled using the scale operator. The effect of this is to multiply the x and y coordinates of each point by a specified amount.

    let s = square (1.0,1.0,1.0)
    let s1 = **scale** s **by** 3.0, 2.0
    let s2 = **scale** s **by** -1.0, 1.0

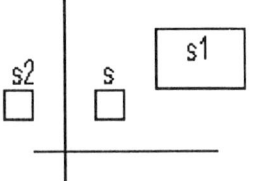

Figure 4.6 The effect of scaling a picture

The **shift** operator may be used to move a picture with respect to the origin

    let s3 = **shift** s **by** 4.0,0.0

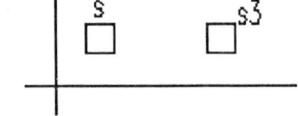

Figure 4.7 The effect of shifting a picture

The **rotate** operator may be used to rotate a picture around the origin. The amount of rotation is given in degrees. The direction of rotation is clockwise.

let s4 = **rotate** s **by** 90

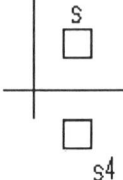

Figure 4.8 The effect of rotation by 90 degrees

It is important to realize that all of the operators discussed so far just act to create values of type **pic**. To actually draw a picture you must output it in some way. There are two possible ways of doing this. Either you send the picture to a plotter, or you convert the abstract picture to a bit-map that can be displayed on a raster graphics device.

In each case a draw procedure must be called of type:

let draw=**proc**({ image or file} device, **pic** to.draw, **real** wx,xy,dx,dy)

The device is either a file that will be sent to the device or a bit-map, the reals wx,wy,dx,dy specify the viewport that is to be used to display the picture.

4.3 PIXELS

There are two ways of representing pictures in computers: as a collection of points or as a bit-map. PS-algol supports the first with the type **pic** and the second with the type **pixel.**

Raster graphics devices use arrays of pixels to represent images. The pixels are the smallest picture element that the display is capable of resolving. In monochrome displays each picture element is either on or off, in colour displays each element can take on one of a finite range of colours. In technical terms this is often implemented by having several colour planes in the display.

In a simple device you may have 3 colour planes each of which drives one of the channels of an RGB monitor. In more advanced displays you may have more planes : up to 24 in the highest quality devices. In these cases the data from the bitplanes is used to control analogue circuitry that modulates the intensity of the colour signals sent out to the display.

An individual pixel will be composed of a bit from each plane. Each of these bits can be either **on** or **off**. To define a one bit pixel in PS-algol you can write:

    let black = **off**
    let white = **on**

The variables black and white are not of type **pixel**. For colour displays we can concatenate **pixels** depthwise:

    let red = **on** & **off** & **off**
    let white = **on** & **on** & **on**

These also have the type **pixel**.

An image is a grid of pixels. As such it has both width and height, and can be declared as follows:

    let red.block := **image** 100 **by** 80 **of** red

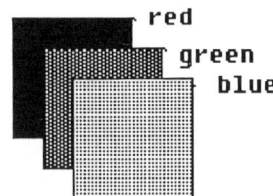

Figure 4.9 An RGB display uses 3 bit planes

This defines red.block to be a rectangle of pixels 100 across by 80 down. The origin is defined to be the bottom left. The type of red.block is **#pixel** the # is intended to give the impression of a grid.

Like any other type images may be passed around as values, and image variables may be updated:

    red.block:=**image** 10 **by** 8 **of** red

There is a predefined **#pixel** on machines with a display called screen. This image corresponds to what is currently being shown on the screen. Other image like red.block are values that are stored in memory and may later be displayed on the screen.

There is an pentadic operator **limit** that enables you to define windows onto the screen or any other device:

let window1 = **limit** screen **to** 100 **by** 50 **at** 30,20

let splodge = **limit** red.block **to** 2 **by** 2 **at** 0,0

Images can be updated using what is referred to as "rasterop". This takes two images and updates the bits of the second image such that each bit in the second image becomes the result of some boolean operation between the bits of the two images. The boolean operations supported are:

ror rand xor copy nand nor not xnor

An example of how to use them is:

copy p1 **onto** p2

Automatic **limit** operations are performed to bring the sizes of the two images into conformity before the update takes place.

4.4 PIXEL MAPPING

There are two special mapping operations that can be used to perform dept wise selection of **pixel**s and **#pixel**s.

red(0)

selects the zeroth bit of the pixel red

screen(1|2)

selects bitplanes 1 and 2 of the screen. Note that bits and bitplanes are indexed from 0.

There are some predefined maps to return the dimensions of an image:

X.dim(**#pixel ->int**)

Y.dim(**#pixel ->int**)

and a map to return the **pixel** at a given position in an image:

Pixel(**#pixel, int, int -> pixel**)

5

Databases and persistence

PS-algol was developed from the language S-algol by applying the principle of orthogonal persistence. This states that any data types that can be handled internally within the language should be storable and transmittable to other programs. No linguistic changes were required to make this extension. All that is involved is an improvement in language implementation technology. There has never been any difficulty storing the base types of programming languages. They can be readily written out to a file and saved for posterity.

The problem came with reference types, **pntr**s in S-algol. These allow the construction of arbitrary graph structures in computer memory. Transferring these to disk has posed implementation problems that most language implementors have ducked. In the next part of the book, techniques for implementing persistence will be gone into in more detail. This chapter will just explain what the programmer sees.

If data is to persist there must be a way in which future programs can refer to data created by past programs. From the programmer's point of view this involves the ability to name data and refer to it in the future. Filing systems provide the traditional way of doing this. A file is a named collection of data. The simplest approach to providing persistence is just to use the filing system to give names to persistent data.

We did not think of this at first, perhaps because we came at the problem from the standpoint of database management systems. Initially we used a database system to store the persistent data, but since I think that the use of a file system is more elegant I will explain that first.

On the MSDOS implementation of PS-algol, all you have to do to save a collection of data is to write a write a pointer to it into a file. The following examples show how it may be done:

```
include ''\salgol\demo\filelib.s''
structure any(int x)
structure cons(pntr hd,tl)

let p =any(4)
write p(x)
let pp:=p
for i=1 to 10 do pp:=cons(any(i),pp)

let f=create(''pntrfile.db'')    ! f is of type file
write '''n file open'n''

output f,pp                      ! output a pointer to the file
close(f)

write '''n file closed'n''
let f2=open(''pntrfile.db'',rmode)    ! reopen the file
let p2 = readp(f2)                    ! read in a pointer
write p2(hd)(x)                       ! check that it has the right data
?
```
        Program readp.s

This writes a pointer to a list of cons cells to a file, closes the file, reopens it, reads back the pointer and checks that it still points at the same thing.

It is not so surprising that this works, you could probably do something similar in Pascal, since the list of cons cells stays in memory throughout the program. If after we have run readp.s we wait a day or two and then run program readp2.s we do something that is beyond the capabilities of most languages.

Ch.5]   DATABASES AND PERSISTENCE   55

include "filelib.s"
structure any(**int** x)
structure cons(**pntr** hd,tl)
let f2=open("pntrfile.db",rmode)
let p2 = readp(f2)
write p2 (hd) (x)
?

    Program readp2.s

    Here we open the previous file, read in the pointer to the list of cons cells and print out the head of the list. Simple is it not?
    In fact, implementing it is horribly complex, but for the programmer it is simple.
    Note that each program must contain declarations of the structure classes used. These are essential for type checking. The run time system checks that the pointer you read back is of the same type as the one you wrote out.
    In Unix implementations it is more complex. The equivalent program would be:

structure any(**int** x)
structure cons(**pntr** hd,tl)

let p =any(4)
write p(x)
let pp:=p
for i=1 **to** 10 **do** pp:=cons(any(i),pp)
let f=create.database("pntrfile.db","pass") ! f is of type pntr to table
s.enter("list",f,p)   ! put p in the table
if commit() = **nil do**
write "'n database closed'n"
let f2=open.database("pntrfile.db","pass","read")   ! reopen the database
let p2 = s.lookup("list",f2)   ! search the table
write p2(hd)(x)   ! check that it has the right data
?
    Program readp.s under unix

The differences between the two implementations are that under Unix special files called databases have to be used. These contain by default a pointer to a table. In the Unix PS-algol tables are implemented as **pntr** values and accessed via a procedure library with calls to procedures called s.enter and s.lookup. The database files have special procedures to open them and a procedure commit must be called to ensure that data is flushed to disk. The assumption that each database will contain a table turns out to be useful for many simple applications. The same effect can be readily mimicked on the MSDOS version.

The following short program maintains a forename/surname database and uses the technique of putting a pointer to a table into a file.

```
include "filelib.s"
structure db($string names)

let t := tab string of
     "Paul":"Cockshott"
     default : " I do not know about them "
write "'n Database demo'n'n1. Open a db'n2. Create new db'n"

 let reply =readi()

case reply of
1 : {
   write "Database file name:"
   let fn= read.a.line()
   let f= open( fn , rmode )
   if f=nullfile then write "Could not open it'n'n'n"
   else {
    let p=readp(f)
      t:=p(names)
   }
 }
2 : write "Using new database 'n"
default : { }

let q:= true
```

```
while q do
begin
   write "'n1. Add a name pair'n'n2. Lookup a surname'n'n3. Quit'n'n>"
   case readi() of
   1 : {
      write "Forename:"
      let f=read.a.line()
      write "Surname:"
      t(f):=read.a.line()
      }
   2 : {
      write "Forename :"
      write t(read.a.line()),'"n"
      }
   default: q:=false
end

write "'n'n'n1. Save Database'n'n2. Quit 'n"
case readi() of
1: {
   write "Dbname:"
   let n=read.a.line()
   let f= create(n)
   if f=nullfile then {
      write " can not open ",n,'"n"
   }
   else
   {
      output f, db(t)
   }
  }
default : write "bye"

?
```

6

The PS-algol abstract machine : scalar variables

Programming languages undergo evolution and so do their implementations. PS-algol is a language in the classic Algol tradition. It is compiled to run on an abstract machine that is also a descendent of the classic Algol abstract machine. An abstract machine is an abstract specification of a computer. This computer can later be built as a real electronic machine or it can be implemented some other way.

6.1 IMPLEMENTATION TECHNIQUES
We can distinguish four main ways of implementing an abstract machine. In ascending order of performance these are:

1. Software interpretation
2. Macro expansion
3. Microcode interpretation
4. Hardware interpretation

The high level language compiler can produce an abstract machine code. For Pascal this code is called P code. For PS-algol it is called S-code.

6.1.1 Software interpretation

If software interpretation is the chosen method then an interpreter program is written in assembly language or in a systems implementation language like C or IMP. This interpreter loads in the abstract machine code and executes it as specified by the abstract machine manual. This is the most common technique used for the implementation of persistent programming languages. It has the

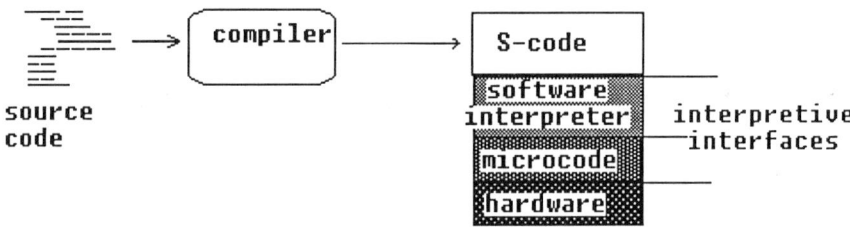

Figure 6.1 Use of a software interpreter

advantage that it is relatively cheap to implement. The implementation can be done by programmers with a medium level of skill. They merely have to be able to translate a specification of the abstract machine into a high level language program. Given a clear specification an experienced C programmer should be able to implement an abstract machine for an Algol-like language in about 6 months. Figure 6.1 illustrates the use of software interpretation as an implementation technique.

6.1.2 Macro expansion

Macro expansion is a higher performance technique. In this the abstract machine code is translated into a series of macro assembly statements of the target machine on which it is intended to run. The translation process is shown in Figure 6.2. In this case the target machine, which might be a Vax will end up executing a machine code program in Vax machine code. Since the intermediate step of software interpretation has been removed, the speed of execution of the final program should be faster. With PS-algol systems, the speedup turns out to be about 3 to 1. Macro expansion is a more demanding technique than software interpretation. It requires a skilled assembly language programmer to do it. The programmer must have an intimate knowledge of the architecture and instruction set of both the abstract machine and the target machine. Considerable care must be taken in the choice of target machine instructions to get the best performance. Since the speed at which assembly level programs can be written and debugged is lower than C programs, it will probably take about twice as long to implement a system using this technique. One also has to consider the fact that you lose portability in going to a macro expanded implementation. A software

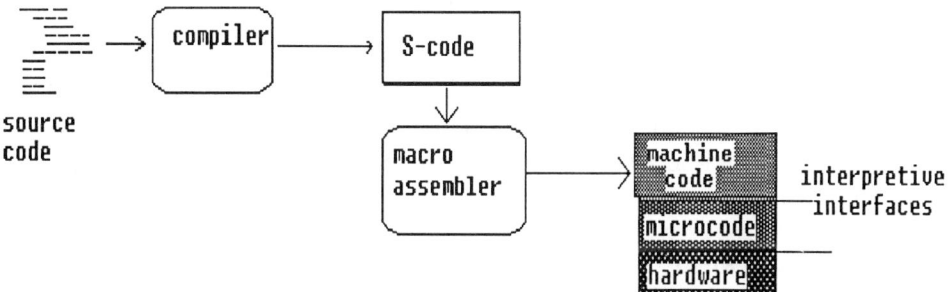

Figure 6.2 Compilation to host machine code

interpreter written in C will work on a wide range of machines with minimal alteration. If you have a macro expansion code generator for the Vax you can only use it on the Vax.

6.1.3 Microcode interpretation

The next step up in the performance ladder is to use a microcoded machine with an interpreter for the abstract machine resident in it as a microprogram. With this sort of approach the abstract machine code of PS-algol or some other persistent programming language should run at the same sort of speed as the native code of other microprogrammed processors like the Vax or the M68000. The use of a microprogrammed interpreter is shown in Figure 6.3. As we go up the performance ladder we find that the cost of implementation goes up. It is much more difficult to find people with microprogramming skills than assembler skills. Even if you can find the programmers, it is difficult to get hold of a microcodable machine. Manufacturers are often loath to allow people outside the company to get their hands on the microcode of their machines. If you do alter the microcode you may find that you no longer have an operating system

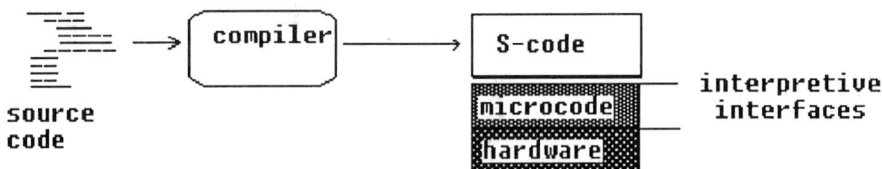

Figure 6.3 Microcode interpretation of S-code

available, since the operating system and the microcode of a computer are highly interdependent. It seems unlikely that it is worthwhile to implement a microcoded machine for a persistent programming language unless you are a computer manufacturer who intends to sell the whole system from hardware to software as an integrated product.

6.1.4 Direct hardware interpretation

Direct hardware interpretation of the abstract machine code is the most difficult and costly alternative. It requires the skills of hardware engineers and a long time scale. It presupposes the resources required to implement not just the hardware but the entire software support environment that will run on that hardware. The process of direct hardware execution is illustrated in Figure 6.4. The recent popularity of RISC processors has encouraged the use of direct hardware interpretation for languages like C and FORTRAN. For a block structured language that supports persistence, the use of similar hardware acceleration techniques is very much a research topic.

Most persistent programming languages are implemented using software interpretation of an abstract machine. This is true of PS-algol on the

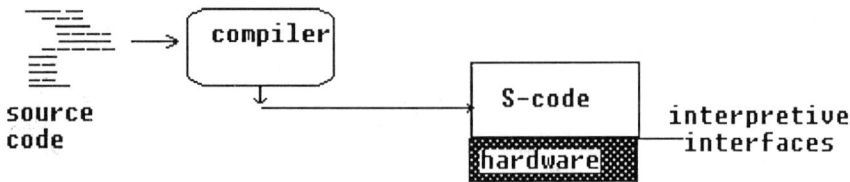

Figure 6.4 Direct hardware execution of S-code

M68000 series, the ICL Perq and Series 39 and for Smalltalk implementations on M68000 series and the IBM PC. On St Andrews PS-algol on the DEC Vax, macro expansion was used but this has not generally been a popular technique. The original Smalltalk system on the Xerox Alto was run on a microprogrammed interpreter and the Royal Signals and Radar Establishment produced a persistent version of Algol68 on a microcoded version of the ICL Perq. Direct hardware support for persistent programming is rare. A possible examples are the SOAR (Smalltalk On A Risc) project at Berkley. The OBJEKT Chipset produced by Linn Products of Glasgow runs a PS-algol system written by the author in which certain low level operations on persistent objects are supported in hardware, with others implemented by a combination of microcode and macro expansion from S-code.

The PS-algol abstract machine that is described below is is the one that was used in the first versions of PS-algol. As the language developed, new features were added to it. This involved the abstract machine becoming more complex. In subsequent chapters we will deal with the evolution of the abstract machine. It is worth doing this because some persistent programming languages will be simpler than the current release of PS-algol and could be implemented using a simple abstract machine like that used in the first versions of PS-algol.

6.2 STORES

An abstract machine specifies a set of stores and a set of operations on these stores. These stores can have a number of possible types. One class of store is predesignated variables capable of holding an individual word of data. We generally call these registers. In an actual hardware machine the registers will often be implemented by using particularly fast memory chips, or in a microprocessor, by using on chip memory cells. From the standpoint of abstract machine design this is not important, since an abstract machine is concerned only with the functional specification of a computer. The speed of access to different parts of the store is an implementation optimization.

Some abstract machines support a random access memory. The PS-algol machine does not. Instead it uses forms of structured memory: stacks and heaps. The organization of the structured memory is at the heart of how persistence works. On a given implementation these may actually be implemented in a common random access store, but this is not necessary. Indeed it might be advantageous from a performance point of view to implement the heaps and stacks as physically distinct memories.

The areas of memory defined by the PS-algol abstract machine are the registers, the code store, the stacks, and the heaps. These are shown diagrammatically in Figure 6.5. It is often easiest to get a general idea of an abstract machine using diagrams like this, but when you are implementing an abstract machine this sort of specification using pictures can be too vague. To avoid this specialized languages have been developed for specifying abstract machines. One of the best known is ISPS (Instruction Set Processor Specification). This is described in Chapter 4 of *Computer Structures* by Siewiorek, Bell & Newell. I will use ISPS notation to describe the PS-algol abstract machine.

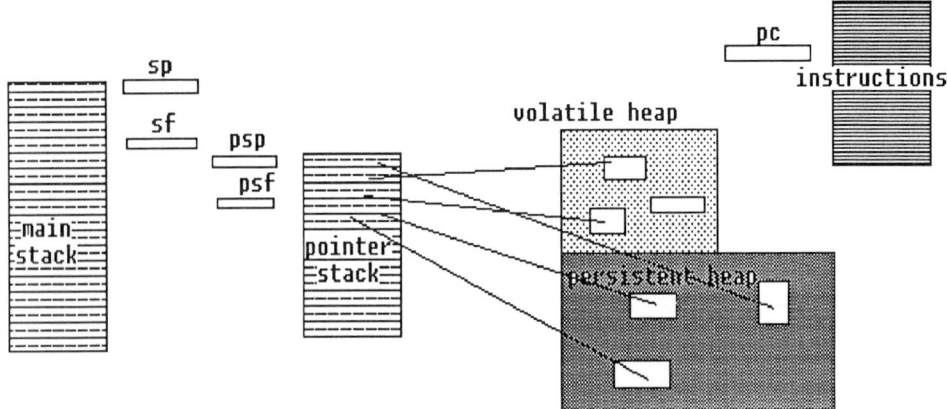

Figure 6.5 Registers and stores of the PS-algol abstract machine

6.3 STACKS

PS-algol, like all Algols is a recursive language. It is recursive in two senses. It is defined by a recursive grammar and it allows the recursive calling of procedures. This imposes special constraints on the store of the language that are best satisfied by a stack structured memory. Consider the fragment of code shown in Example 6.1.. In this example four variables are define **a,i,x,y**, but at no point are more than 3 of the variables in scope at once. At position 2 the variables **x,y,a** are in scope and at position 3 the variables **x,y,i** are in scope. In other words, different variables persist for different periods of time. Variables are only in scope between the point at which they are declared and the end of the block. Because the grammar of Algol allows blocks to be nested it generates a Last In First Out discipline on the scope rules. The variables in the outermost

```
begin
    let x:=3
    let y:=x*readi
! position 1
    begin
        let a = x
        x:=y; y:=a
! position 2
    end
    begin
        let i:=9+x
        if i>y do y:=x
! position 3
    end
end
```

Example 6.1

block remain in scope for the entire program whereas the variables in innermost blocks are discarded first. This lends itself naturally to a stack implementation.

The PS-algol code in Example 6.1 would be equivalent to the S-code in Example 6.2.

The evolution of the stack during this process is shown in Figure 6.6. It can be seen that the S-code uses postfix notation. Arguments are pushed onto the stack and then operated on. Variables are accessed by specifying their address relative to the bottom of the stack. The variable **x** is accessed using the operator **global(0)** since it is at the base of the stack, **y** is addressed as **global(1)** as it is at position 1 on the stack etc. It is worth noting that the combination of the PS-algol initializing assignment statement

    let <variable>:= <expression>

with the stack allocation discipline means that many of the store instructions that would be required in a conventional machine architecture are dispensed with. The initial value is simply calculated and then left on the stack. The compiler then just remembers where on the stack it was left.

6.3.1 Main stack

The main stack of the PS-algol abstract machine is an array of words. These words are addressed via a pair of registers: the stack pointer or SP register and the Stack Frame or SF register. In ISPS formalism we can express this as

```
 1       ll.int(3)            ! let x:=3
 2       global(0)             ! x -> top of stack
 3       readi                 ! readi -> top of stack
 4       times                 ! let y:= x*readi
! position 1
 5       global(0)             ! let a=x
 6       globaladdr(0)         ! addr(x) -> top of stack
 7       global(1)             ! y -> top of stack
 8       assign.op             ! x:=y
 9       globaladdr(1)         ! addr(y)->top of stack
10       global(2)             ! a-> top of stack
11       assign.op             ! y:=a
! position 2
12       retract(1)            ! get rid of a
13       ll.int(9)             ! 9 -> top of stack
14       global(0)             ! x-> top of stack
15       plus                  ! let i:=9+x
16       global(2)             ! i->top of stack
17       global(1)             ! y->top of stack
18       lt.i                  ! i<y -> top of stack
19       jumpf(23)             ! if top of stack
                               ! false goto 23
20       globaladdr(0)         ! addr(x) -> top of stack
21       global(1)             ! y -> top of stack
22       assign.op             ! x:=y
!  position 3
23       retract(1)            ! get rid of i
24       retract(2)            ! get rid of x and y
```

Example 6.2

** Main Stack state **
MS\Main.Stack[0:StackMax]<0..31>,
SP\Stack.Pointer<0..31>,
SF\Stack.Frame<0..31>,
   TOS\Top.Of.Stack<0..31>   := MS[SP]<0..31>,
   NOS\Next.Of.Stack<0..31>   := MS[SP-1]<0..31>,
    FTOS\Floating.point.TOS<0..64> := MS[SP-1:SP]<0..31>,
   FNOS\Floating.point.NOS<0..64> := MS[SP-3:SP-2]<0..31>

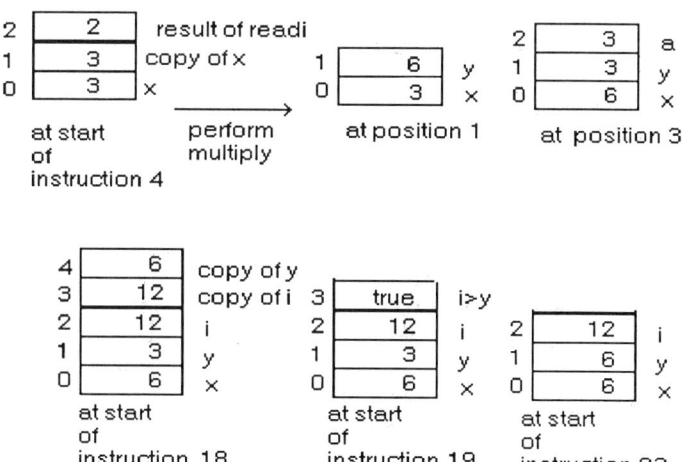

Figure 6.6 The evolution of the stack during example 6.2

This indicates that the main stack is an array of 32 bit words, and that the stack pointer and stack frame registers are individual 32 bit words.

All arithmetic and logical operations on integers and booleans take place between the top two items of stack and have the general form:

NOS = TOS op NOS next
SP = SP - 1

with the obvious extension for floating point operands.

6.3.2 Procedure calls

The most complicated part of the stack in an Algol-based language is the way in which it is used to implement procedure calls. We have explained how the use of algol scope rules combined with first class functions can provide a module-like capability to a language. To support this requires a complex procedure call discipline. The first release of PS-algol did not support first class procedures, but it did allow procedures to be passed as parameters to other procedures. This is quite a difficult feature to implement.

Example 6.3 illustrates this. This deals with the problem of performing a search on a binary tree. The nodes of the tree contain strings but the rule for comparing strings can not be straight forward. In some circumstances it might be appropriate just to sort the strings in lexicographic order. In others a more

```
structure tree(string node,datum; pntr left,right)
let search = proc( pntr to.tree;
            proc(string,string->int) compare;
            string key
          -> string )
  if to.tree = nil then ''''
  else case compare(to.tree(node),key) of
      -1    : search(to.tree(right),compare, key)
       0    : to.tree(datum)
    default : search(to.tree(left), compare, key)
```

Example 6.3 a parameterized search procedure

complex rule has to be used. If the strings were lists of names and addresses in the form:

    James Anderson, 112 King Street
    Heather Paterson, 12 Vicar Rd

then lexicographic ordering on the strings would end up sorting people in order of their first names rather than their surnames. If the strings actually contained numbers in decimal or octal notation, then the sensible thing to do would be to sort them in terms of ascending numeric value. One way to do this would be to parameterize the search procedure with a string comparison function.

The search procedure takes as a parameter a procedure compare that returns -1, 0 or 1 depending on whether the result of comparison is less than, equal to or greater than. By supplying appropriate versions of the compare procedure a whole variety of different types of strings can be put into a sorted tree.

To take the case of sorting strings on the basis of surnames. The surname must be extracted from the string before comparison is made. The extraction procedure will have to know the characters that delimit the surname to the left and the right. We could package this up by writing a procedure that searched trees ordered on surnames. This is illustrated in Example 6.4.

The search.surname procedure might be called by passing in the details of how to distinguish a surname

    search.surname(a.tree,"James Anderson", " ", ",")

```
let extract.string = proc(string name,left,right ->string)
begin
    let start=find.substr(name,left)
    let finish=find.substr(name,right)
    name(start+1|finish-start -1)
end

let search.surname = proc(pntr to.tree;
                          string key,left.delim,right.delim
                          ->string)
begin
    let compare.surname = proc( string s1,s2 ->int)
    begin
        let name1=extract.string(s1,left.delim,right.delim)++s1
        let name2=extract.string(s2,left.delim,right.delim)++s2
        if name1<name2 then -1
        else if name1=name2 then 0
        else 1
    end
    search(to.tree,compare.surname,key)
end
```

Example 6.4 parameterizing the search procedure

The problem is to devise a calling mechanism that will:

a) Enable procedures to have space for local variables
b) Allow these to be called recursively

c) Allow procedures to access variables that are in a surrounding scope

d) enable procedures like procedure **compare.surname** to correctly access the left and right delimiter strings **left.delim** and **right.delim**. At the point where compare surname is called inside **search** these variables are not in scope.

The local variables of a procedure are addressed by specifying an offset

Figure 6.7 The use of the SF and the
SP registers to address the stack

from the stack frame register. Figure 6.7 shows how this is done. On entry into a procedure the old value of the stack frame is stored on the stack along with the return address. This stored version of the SF register is termed the dynamic link. When a return instruction is executed the old value of the SF is restored from the dynamic link. This restores the addressing environment for the local variables of the called procedure. The new value of the SF register points just above the stack frame. The procedure's parameters and variables are then addressed with positive offsets from the SF register. Strictly speaking the SF register is unnecessary. It would be possible to implement the same process by using negative offsets from the SP register.

All of the above mechanisms could be used in languages like C which have recursive procedures but which are not block structured. Block structured languages have the additional problem of having to address variables that are neither local nor global but of intermediate scope.

From within the procedure compare.name the variables left.delim and right.delim are of intermediate scope. PS-algol uses a mechanism called a static chain to access these variables. When a procedure is declared, the procedure variable is initialized. The value with which it is initialized is termed a closure. The closure comprises two parts : a pointer to the start address of the procedure code and a pointer to the environment in which the procedure is declared. This closure is the value of the procedure. If a procedure is passed into another procedure as a parameter, as is the case with compare name, then it is the procedure closure that is actually put on the stack as a parameter.

When a procedure is called the sequence following is carried out:

1. push the procedure closure

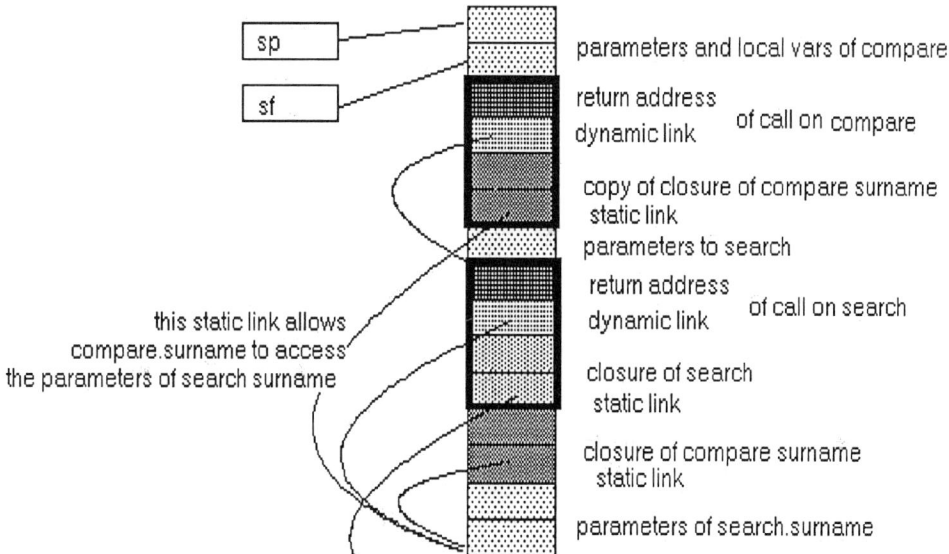

Figure 6.8 This shows how the use of procedure closures and a static link enables a procedure to access the environment in which it was declared

2. leave space for the return address and dynamic link

3. evaluate the parameters and leave on stack

4. store the SF in the dynamic link

5. store the return address in the stack

6. update the SF to point at base of the parameters

7. branch to the code address given in the closure

This gives rise to the stack organization shown in Figure 6.8. The variables of search.surname can be accessed from within the body of the procedure compare.surname by following the static link.

The addressing modes necessary to get at the different classes of variables - local, global and intermediate - can be summarized in the ISPS specification in Example 6.5. An intermediate addressing instruction takes two parameters, a lexical level and an offset. The lexical level specifies how many levels down the static link chain it is necessary to go to find the frame that contains the variables you want.

This process could be rather slow since it includes a loop that chases down the chain. In practice this is not found to be a problem because intermediate variables are actually accessed much less often than global or local variables. For most variable accesses the effective address can be computed just on the basis of the instruction and the SF register. An alternative technique for handling block structured languages on general register machines uses a display or collection of registers pointing at the stack frames that correspond to successive lexical levels. As each lexical level is entered a CPU register is set aside to point at the start of the variables of that lexical level. This technique has the advantage that the CPU can compute the effective address without following a static chain by simply using base and offset addressing modes, but as against this it makes the implementation of procedure calling more difficult.

When a procedure is called the old display must be saved on the stack and a new display constructed for the environment that is being entered. It seems doubtful that this is worthwhile. With a display an overhead will be encountered on every procedure call, even though most procedures only use local or global variables and so have no need of a display. Unless a processor has special fast instructions for manipulating displays on procedure entry and exit, then the use of static links is to be preferred.

```
** instruction decode registers **
IR\instruction.register<0..7>,
OR\offset.register<0..15>,
LL\lexical.level.register<0..7>,
SL\static.link.register<0..31>,

** address mode register **
am<0..1>,
EA\Effective.Address<0..31>:=
    begin
    decode am=>
        begin
        0 : EA = OR      ! global access
```

```
      1 : EA = SF + OR    ! local access
      2 : EA = Chain +OR  ! intermediate address
      end
   end,
chain\follows.static.chain<0..31>:=
   begin
   SL = SF -2 next
   WHILE LL > 0
      begin
      SL = SL -2 ; LL = LL -1
      end
   end
```

Example 6.5 effective address evaluation

7

Object store

Ps-algol uses both object and value semantics.

Values are abstractions. The value 2 for instance is an abstraction that subsumes all concrete pairs of things. This characteristic of being abstract makes it atemporal. The number 2 is neither created not destroyed. As an atemporal abstraction it cannot be changed. You cannot increment the value 2. You can increment a program variable that contains the value 2, but what this does is to cause the variable to point at the number 3 rather than the number 2.

The language Algol68 used a rather long winded, if precise, notation to describe this. The **mode** of the number 2 is an **int** in Algol68 whereas the **mode** of an integer variable is a **ref int**. The notion conveyed here is that the variable refers to an integer. Which integer it refers to may change if an assignment operation is performed. But the integers themselves remain unaffected by the assignment. If the variable **x** originally contains 2 then the expression **x plus 1**, will cause **x** to contain 3 but this does not alter the value of any other variable which may have contained 2.

In PS-algol certain data types are always treated as values. They are the types **int, real, bool, string** and **pic**. These types correspond to sets of values. Each set has base members and an algebra from which the other members of the set can be derived. For the integers the base members are **0** and **1** and the other integers can be derived by means of addition and subtraction. For the type string the base elements are the set of single element ISO character strings. All other members of the type string can be generated form this base set by the operation ++ (string concatenation). The base members of the set of pictures are the set of all points in Euclidian space. The generative operations are joining, scaling, rotating and translating.

From the point of view of persistence pure values are not very interesting. Since they are atemporal they exist without the help of computers. We do not need any special computer technology to preserve the **number** 1. What raises the issue of persistence are updateable locations that can take on different values through time. These locations are at the heart of object semantics.

An object has state. Its state is the value or set of values that it contains. This may change over time. Assignment operations allow state to be changed. An object such as an array has duration. It comes into existence at a particular point in the execution and persists for a period after. During that period elements of the array may be updated. The array itself persists even while its values change.

The main types of object supported in PS-algol are vectors, structures and images (which are two dimensional arrays of pixels). Something that distinguishes PS-algol from languages like Pascal or C is that the sizes of these arrays and structures may not be known at compile time. A vector may be generated by a vector expression of the form:

vector <expression>::<expression> **of** <expression>

In this expression the type of the elements of the vector is specified at compile time but the bounds of the vector my be computed at run time, e.g.:

let b := **vector** 1 ::i **of** 0.0

At compile time all that is known is that **b** will refer to a vector of reals with lower bound 1. This means that the compiler cannot arrange to reserve space for the vector. Instead some run time mechanism must allocate the necessary space. This rules out the technique used for arrays in many other programming languages where a fixed number of words on the stack would be reserved for the variable **b** by the compiler.

Another complication is introduced by the object semantics of PS-algol. It is possible for two variables to refer to the same array. In Example 7.1 the answer printed out will be 10, because both vector variables refer to the same object: the vector created on line 1.

let a := @ 1 **of int** [1,2,4,8]
let b := a
a(1) := 10
write b(1)

Example 7.1

The implication of this is that vector variables must be implemented as pointers to the actual vector objects. Assignment of the value of one vector variable to another vector variable can then be performed by copying the pointer not copying the vector object. This is already implied in the case of structures since the variables that refer to them are declared to be of type **pntr**.

7.1 P STACK

All variables of type **pntr, vector, image, string** and **pic** are implemented as pointers. Variables of these pointer types are allocated on a second stack the P stack. The P stack requires another two registers to implement it. These are the pointer stack pointer or PSP and the pointer stack frame or PSF register. These are used in a way that is analogous to the SP and SF registers.

The variables on the P stack are in the form of pointers that point into two areas of store called the volatile heap and the persistent heap. Expressions which create heap objects, like vectors or structures, cause space to be reserved for an

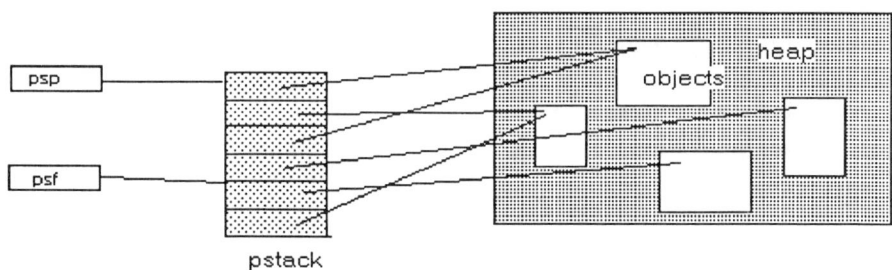

Figure 7.1 The P-stack contains pointers to objects on the heap

object in one of the volatile heap. A pointer to the newly created object is returned on the top of the P stack. Example 7.2 shows how the PS-algol in Example 7.1 would be implemented.

7.2 THE VOLATILE HEAP

The volatile heap is an area of memory used to create objects that have been dynamically created during the course of the program or objects that have been brought in from a database during the course of a program. In most implementations of PS-algol the objects on the heap are directly referred to by their addresses which are stored on the P stack. In some implementations the pointers are stored as tokens on the P stack and some form of mapping is interposed between the stack and the heap. The general arrangement is shown in Figure 7.1.

7.2.1 Garbage Collection

A stack provides an automatic mechanism for claiming and releasing storage space. As a procedure executes the stack grows with the values pushed on it. On exit from a procedure the stack is retracted releasing the space used during the procedure. With a heap it is not possible to use this simple mechanism. Suppose we have a function that returns a vector as a result. It might for instance read in a list of real numbers and return them as a *real. Since the length of the list is not initially known the vector must be extended as new numbers are read in. A possible algorithm is given in Example 7.3.

```
let read.list = proc(->*real)
begin
    let initial.vector = vector 1::1 of readr
    let n := 1
    let vec := initial.vector
    while not eoi do
    begin
        n := n + 1
        let vec2 := vector 1::n of readr
        for i= 1 to n-1 do vec2(i):=vec(i)
        vec:=vec2
    end
    vec
end
```

Example 7.3 A function to read in a list of reals

Ch.7]   OBJECT STORE   79

```
! let a := @1 of int [ 1 , 2, 3, 4]
    ll.int(1)       ! push the lower bound
                    ! of the vector

    ll.int(1)
    ll.int(2)
    ll.int(4)
    ll.int(8)   ! push the initial
                ! values of the vector on
                ! the main stack
    make.vector.ib(5)
        ! form a vector from the top 5 words
        ! on the main stack
        ! result returns on P stack as a
! let b:=a
    p.global(0)
! a(1):=10
    p.global(0) ! push a on p stack
    ll.int(1)   ! push 1 on m stack
    ll.int(10)  ! push 10 on m stack
    subvass.ib  ! perform the assignment
! write b(1)
    p.global(1) ! push b on p stack
    ll.int(1)   ! push 1 on m stack
    subv.ib     ! subscript the vector
    write.op
```

Example 7.2

In this new vectors are repeatedly created, each one larger than the last. The old vector is then copied into the first n-1 elements of the new vector which then becomes the current vector. It is not perhaps the most efficient way of building up a vector from an arbitrary length list but it is simple and it works. It is obviously the case that a lot of store is used up by the algorithm since vectors keep being created and then their pointers are overwritten. A little thought shows that store used will be proportional to $n^2/2$ so that for a long list it will rapidly exhaust the space available on the volatile heap.

Suppose the volatile heap occupied 64K bytes and we had to read in a list of 1024 reals. Assuming that reals occupy 64 bits, we would need only about 8K for the final vector, but the total space claimed for vectors during the algorithm would be $1024*1024*8/2 = 4$ megabytes. This would far exhaust the space on the heap. In fact the heap will be exhausted after 128 reals have been read in. This is unsatisfactory. Some mechanism has to be invoked to recover the space taken up by all those temporary vectors which are no longer needed.

This process of storage recovery is called garbage collection because the temporary vectors are just rubbish that clutter up the store. Garbage collection determines which vectors are rubbish and reuses the space that they occupy. Garbage collection has long been a standard feature of functional languages like Lisp but for some reason it has been less common in imperative languages. Most Pascal and C implementations still make do with antediluvian heaps with no garbage collectors. Among imperative languages it has been the Algol family (algolW, Algol68, PS-algol) that have developed garbage collectors.

The basic task of a garbage collector is to discard all objects on the heap that will not be needed for future computation and can never be used again in the program. In practice implementors of garbage collectors are willing to settle for slightly less stringent aims:

> 1) All objects that can be referred to at a later point in the program must be retained

> 2) As many as possible of the remaining objects must be discarded and their space made available for future use.

The rule used in PS-algol implementations is that **all objects that are directly referred to by variables that are in scope or are indirectly reachable from these by following chains of pointers must be retained.**

This rule is imperfect since it may result in a certain number of objects being retained that will never be accessed again. If garbage collection takes place in the middle of the **for** loop in Example 7.3 , then the store occupied by **initial.vector** will be retained even though it is never referred to again in the program. This is a minor problem and the rule gives results which are quite acceptable in practice.

We can now see the justification for the two stacks used in the abstract machine. The set of pointer variables that are in scope is identical with the P-stack. Every pointer variable that could possibly be referred to will be on the P-stack. It is a simple task for the garbage collector to scan the P-stack and retain all of the things that it points at. If the pointer variables were stored on the main

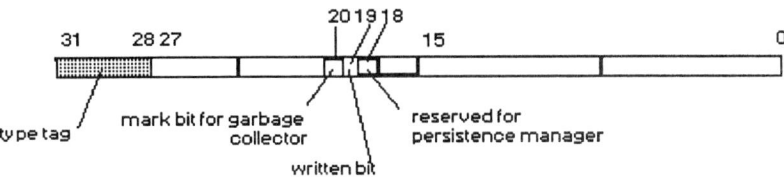

Figure 7.2 The header word of a heap object

stack along with the integers, reals etc then it would be necessary for the garbage collector to have a means of distinguishing between pointers and other variables. This is not impossible. There are several obvious and some not so obvious ways in which this could be done, but the use of a distinct stack for pointers to heap objects has an elegant simplicity.

7.2.2 Objects on the Heap
The use of a P-stack enables the garbage collection software to find all of the variables in scope that point to heap objects. The second problem is to find all of the objects that are directly or indirectly referred to by objects that are in scope. This means that it must be possible for the garbage collector to recognize the type of objects on the heap. If it encounters a vector of vectors it must know to keep all of the sub-vectors that it points to, or conversely if it encounters a string on the heap it will know that this will contain no further pointers and so its contents can be ignored for garbage collection purposes. This gives rise to the requirement that objects on the heap be self describing. Each object must have a marker or header that identifies its type to the garbage collector and enables the garbage collector to discover where its internal pointers are. All heap objects in the standard PS-algol abstract machine have a header word that is shown in Figure 7.2.

7.2.3 Strings
Strings have the structure shown in Figure 7.3. The only information stored in the header of a string is its length. This is different from the convention in C of a null terminated string. Storing the length of a string as a distinct integer has the advantage that the length function can be implemented efficiently. It also allows the character code 0 to be included in the characterset of the language. The abstract machine allows strings of length up to 64k characters.

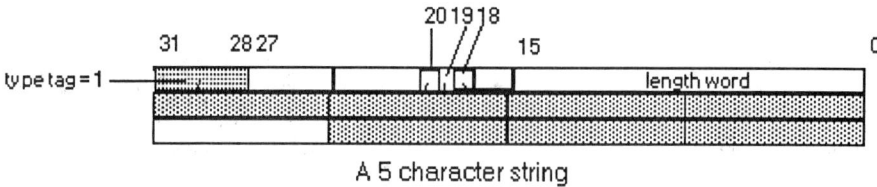

Figure 7.3 The format of a string on the heap

7.2.4 Images

Images have the structure shown in Figure 7.4. Their structure is more complicated than that of a string. Since an image can be part of a larger image, it is necessary to separate the bitmap containing the information about the image from the image as a conceptual object. The image structure effectively defines a window onto the bitmap. The first field after the header points at a vector of bitmap vectors, one for each colour plane. The X and Y offsets and the X and Y dimensions of the image define the image within the bitmaps.

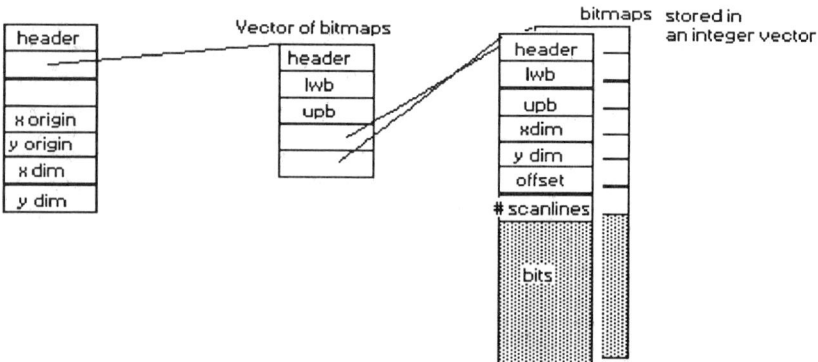

Figure 7.4 An image datastructure on the heap

Table 7.1 Image object

word	meaning
0	header
1	pointer to vector of bitmaps
2	reserved
3	X offset into bitmap
4	Y offset into bitmap
5	X dimension of image
6	Y dimension of image

Table 7.2 Bitmap Vector

word	meaning
0	header format for an integer vector
1	lower bound of an integer vector
2	upper bound of an integer vector
3	X dimension of bitmap
4	Y dimension of bitmap
5	Offset to start of image from start of object. This field allows access to the screen bitmap it may be at some fixed address
6	Number of scan lines per screen page
7...	Bits

7.2.5 Vectors

The format of vectors is shown in Figure 7.5. The PS-algol abstract machine includes the upper and lower bounds of the vector within the vector itself. This

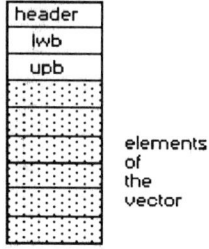

Figure 7.5 Format of a vector on the heap

is required since the bounds of a vector are not in general known at compile time. When a vector is subscripted the index is checked against these bounds and a run time error is generated if the index is out of bounds.

7.2.6 Structures

The process of making data objects self describing goes one step further with the representation of structures. PS-algol uses a combination of run time with compile time type checking. At compile time, checks are performed to ensure that only valid operations are performed on the base types like integers, reals and pointers. It is also possible to check that only vectors are subscripted with integers and that the correct types of parameters are passed to procedures. The run time type checks are introduced by the generic pointer type. This can refer to any class of structure. When a pointer dereference is performed, the compiler can deduce from the fieldname used what class the program assumes is being pointed at.

```
structure cons(pntr hd,tl)
structure int.container(int int.val)
structure string.container(string string.val)

let printlist :=proc(pntr list);{}
printlist :=proc(pntr list)
if list ~= nil do begin
    if list(hd) is string.container do write list(hd,string.val)
        if list(hd) is int.container do write list(hd,int.val)
    printlist(list(tl))
end
```

Example 7.4 A procedure to print a list of integers or strings

For this polymorphism to be both useful and safe it is necessary for the program to be able to specify run time type checks on pointers to see what a pointer points to. A number of different techniques are possible for this. In S-algol, which is similar to PS-algol but lacks persistence, the technique used was to label each instance of a structure class with an integer called the trademark. The compiler assigned different integers to each structure class so that in the example a cons might have trademark 1, an int.container a trademark of 2 etc. At run time the is operation was implemented by a check to see what integer was contained in the first slot in the structure.

For a persistent language in which programs are independently compiled and then linked to databases that contain structures produced by previous programs this will not work. If we have two programs which use the same structure classes but which declare them in a different order then their trademarks will be inconsistent. Cons cells generated by program A might not be recognized as such by program B. To get round this the PS-algol system replaces the integer trademarks by strings as shown in Figure 7.6. The strings contain a canonical representation of the structure declaration: the effect of running the structure declaration through a pretty printer.

String comparisons can be more costly than integer comparisons. But an optimization helps to take care of this. Since strings in the abstract machine are implemented as pointers to strings on the heap, string comparison can be preceded by a pointer comparison. If the two strings are at the same address on the heap their contents are bound to be the same. Pointer comparison can be as cheap as integer comparison. The great majority of implicit is operators will succeed. They must since the first one to fail aborts the program. If all instances of a structure class point at the same copy of the trademark string and if this copy is used in the is operation, then one can be guaranteed that checks will normally run fast.

Only when an object is brought in from another database is there the need to perform a full string comparison.

Another feature of the organization of the structures on the heap is that the fields declared in the program are rearranged in the heap representation so

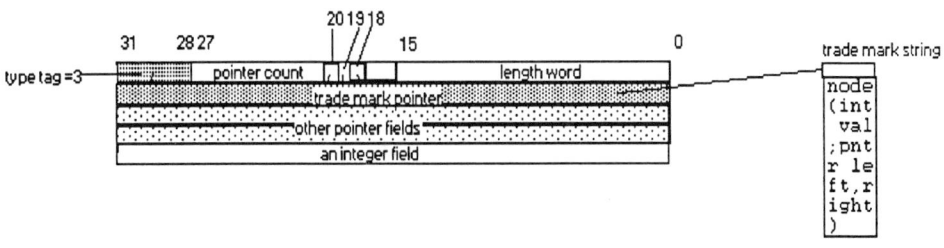

Figure 7.6 the format of a structure on the heap

that all of the pointers come at the front of a structure. A count is provided in the beginning of the structure saying how many pointers are present. This allows the garbage collector to rapidly find all of the pointers going out from a structure. In this case as in others the term pointer will refer not only to pointers to structures but also pointers to other heap objects like strings and vectors.

7.3 THE IDEA OF A PERSISTENT IDENTIFIER (PID)

Conventional heap technology uses store addresses to point at objects. This is a natural outgrowth of the use of random access memory computers, but it is a rather low level approach. It fails to distinguish between the abstract properties of a pointer and a particular implementation technique.

Abstractly a pointer is an object that will support certain high level operations. In strongly typed languages there are generally three of these:

    a) Pointer equality (pntr,pntr -> bool)
    b) Subscription (pntr,int -> value)
    c) Subscript assignment (pntr, int, value ->void)

In subscription and subscript assignment the integer specifies an offset into the object. The particular implementation of the pointer type does not matter to these operations but it does have a bearing on another implicit property of pointers: their persistence. The persistence or atemporal validity of pointers is assumed implicitly in programming languages. It is assumed that if the following sequence of operations is performed then the persistence constraint will be true:

Persistence constraint

    let p be a pointer
    let i be an integer constant
    let v be some constant value
    subscriptassign(p,i,v) at time t1
    then at time t2 subscript(p,i) = v

Provided that between instant t1 and t2 no other assignment has occurred to (p,i). For non-persistent languages this condition does not hold. If a pointer is written to a file by one Pascal program and read back by another the persistence constraint is not preserved. This is because the pointers are just RAM addresses and the RAM may have been overwritten by other programs in the intervening period.

The key to the implementation of persistent programming languages is to devise a representation of pointers for which the persistence constraint is preserved.

In PS-algol abstract machines the class of pointers for which the persistence constraint is preserved are termed Persistent IDentifiers or PIDs. A PID is a bitstring that is mapped to non-volatile storage and which supports the operations of equality, subscription and subscript assignment persistently. There exist a number of quite distinct ways of implementing PIDs and of incorporating them into abstract machines. In what follows different implementations of PIDs will be looked at in some detail.

Pointer = Union(PID, Address)

In many PS-algol implementations the abstract machine type pointer is actually implemented as a union of two lower level types:

> **PIDs** which are provided by a special purpose database abstract machine
>
> **Addresses** which are provided by the operating system + hardware on which the PS abstract machine runs.

This can be seen diagrammatically in Figure 7.7. As is common with union types, the members of the union are distinguished by the tags. Just as in seaside postcards in the Union between England and Scotland the Scots can be distinguished by their tammys and the English by their bowlers, PIDs and addresses are distinguished by their tops. The most significant bit of a PID is set and of an address it is reset. If in the course of a subscription operation a PID is encountered a call is made on the database machine to fetch the object in question onto the heap. The database machine then overwrites the top of the pointer stack with the address at which it has loaded the object so that the operation can proceed.

If we consider the set of pointers that are on the stack and within objects

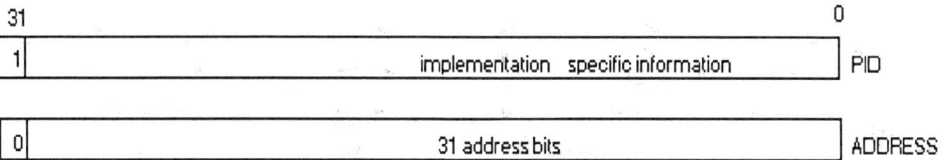

Figure 7.7 Pointers are implemented either as PIDs or ADDRESSes

on the heap these can be divided into three subsets.

> **Subset 1** addresses of objects on the heap created by the current program.

> **Subset 2** PIDs referring to objects within the database created by previous programs.

```
*** POINTER ABSTACT MACHINE ***
H\Heap[0:Heap.Max]<0..31>
PS\Pointer.Stack[0:StackMax]<0..31>
PSP\Pointer.Stack.Pointer<0..31>
PSF\Pointer.Stack.Frame<0..31>
PR\Pointer.Register<0..31>
OR\Offset.Register<0..31>
   PF\Pid.Flag                  :=PR<31>
   PTOS\Pointer.Top.Of.Stack<0..31>  :=PS[PSP]<0..31>
*** Primitive Operations ***
SUBS\Subscript.tos:=
   begin
      PR =PTOS next
      DECODE PF =>
         begin
         0 := SUBS = H[PR+OR]
         1 := begin
            fetch.obj() next
            PR = PTOS next
            SUBS = H[PR+OR]
            end
         end next
      PSP = PSP-1
   end
```

Example 7.5 ISPS description of pointer dereference operation

Subset 3 PIDs referring to objects created by previous programs which have already been loaded onto the heap.

In order to prevent redundant fetches of objects from the database that are already present on the heap a data structure is maintained that keeps track of where objects are.

This data structure is called the Pidlam, which stands for PID to local address map. Conceptually it is a relation of tuples of the form <PID, local address>. In implementation terms it is desirable to be able to rapidly find the local address associated with a PID if the object associated with it has already been entered into the RAM. This can be achieved through providing an auxiliary hash table that indexes the Pidlam by hashing on the PID fields of the tuples.

7.4 MODIFICATION TO GARBAGE COLLECTION

It is necessary to modify the garbage collection algorithm somewhat to take into account the existence of objects that have been brought in from disk. Previously we said that the garbage collector retained all the objects that were reachable from the stack.

This is no longer sufficient. Suppose that we were to bring in from the database a linked list of numbers and that our program moved down the list incrementing every second number on the list. By the time the list was traversed, we might no longer have a pointer to the heap of the list. This would mean that the list was no longer reachable from the stack. If a garbage collection occurred, then the whole list would be discarded. If this happened then our updates to the numbers on the list would be lost to subsequent programs and the persistence constraint would have been violated.

To avoid this it is necessary to retain all objects on the heap that are reachable from either the stack or the Pidlam. This is a very minor modification to a garbage collector.

7.5 IMPLEMENTING THE COMMIT OPERATION

When a commit operation is triggered the language semantics require that the database be updated to contain all the changes that have been made since the start of the program. The first implication of this is that all objects that have been brought in from the database and then modified, must be sent back to the disk. Since the Pidlam contains a complete list of which items have been brought in from disk this can be used to specify which then get written back.

```
export ( pointer)
   if pointer is pid then
      if pointer in pidlam do
      begin
         let la := local.address(pointer)
         if not marked(la) do begin
            mark(la)
            for i = first.pointer(la) to last.pointer(la) do
            la(i) := export(la(i))
         end
      end
   else
      export( allocate.pid.to(pointer) )

commit
   begin
      for each <pid,la> in pidlam do export(pid)
      for each <pid,la> in pidlam do
         if modified(la) then write.to.disk(pid,la)
   end
```

Example 7.6 The commit algorithm

Only some of the items referred to by the Pidlam will actually have been modified. If everything listed on the Pidlam were sent back to disk the commit operation might be unduly slow. This would particularly affect sessions which were query dominated rather than update dominated. In these cases, a lot of unnecessary information would be written to disk. To avoid this PS-algol implementations maintain a written bit in the head of all objects. If an object is modified, then the written bit is set. The commit procedure then only sends back to disk those objects that have been changed since they were brought in. An obvious corollary of this is that the written bits on objects must be cleared as they are written out to disk so that subsequent sessions can tell if they are modified again.

In addition to writing out to disk all of the objects that have been modified since they were imported the commit procedure may have to write to disk some newly created objects that have been linked in to existing persistent objects. This is the way the whole of the persistent database is built up. At the start of the session a single persistent object, the root table is brought in from disk. Arbitrary directed graphs can then be hung onto the root table and at commit time they will be written out to disk. This is achieved by converting all addresses within objects to PIDs before writing the object out to disk. If in the process it is found that an object does not have a PID (i.e., it was created during this session) it is allocated one and then treated just like an imported object. This can be summarized in the procedure export shown in Example 7.6.

It is necessary to discover whether an object that is to be written out to disk has already got a PID. If it has not it must be allocated one. This requires a means of mapping from local addresses to PIDs, the inverse of the normal Pidlam mapping. This can be achieved either by maintaining a secondary hash table in the Pidlam indexed on local addresses or by planting after each object on the heap a pointer to its Pidlam entry. In the case of objects without a PID this pointer will be nil. This arrangement is shown in Figure 7.8.

7.6 THE INTERFACE TO THE PERSISTENT HEAP

Objects have to be transferred between the volatile and the persistent heap. It has been found that there is a small set of primitive operations on the persistent heap that are sufficient for this. These are invoked by the run time system of the language on an underlying layer of software that maintains the persistent heap

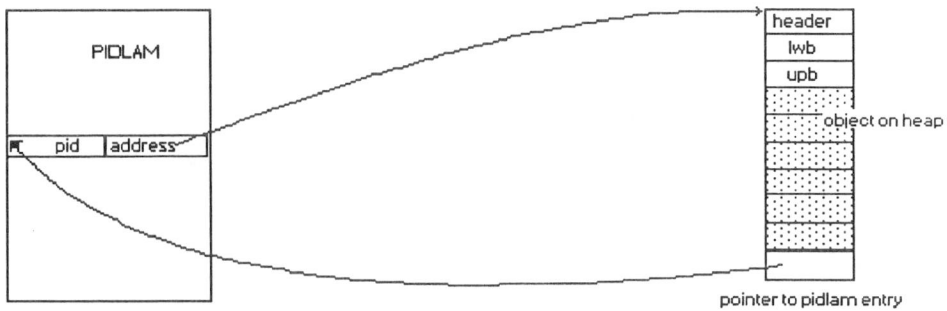

Figure 7.8 Objects have back pointers to their PIDLAM entries

on disk. The names of the routines vary between implementations but their functionality remains essentially the same.

>   Open.database(name,mode -> root.pid)

This opens the database in the requested mode and returns the PID of the root object. By convention in PS-algol a structure of class table is stored in the root object.

>   get.size(pid ->size)

This tells the volatile heap system how bit an object on disk so that space can be reserved in RAM for it.

>   get.chunk(pid,buffer.address)

This reads an object into RAM at the buffer address.

>   put.chunk(pid,buffer.address)

This causes the object at buffer.address to be transferred to disk into the slot reserved for the object with the given pid.

>   create.chunk(size->pid)

This creates a slot in the persistent heap to hold an object and returns a PID referring to it.

>   commit.database(name)

This closes the database, makes sure all buffers are flushed to disk and ensures that the disk representation is in a consistent state.

8

Disk organization

PS-algol systems have to organize two types of storage media, the RAM and the disk. In this they differ from other language implementations which just have to organize a single store, the RAM. Disk store is unlike RAM. Its access speed is lower by some 5 orders of magnitude. Its word size is large : typically 4096 bits. It is non-volatile. This means that different techniques have to be used to organize it.

PS-algol systems maintain two heaps. We have already talked about the heap in RAM. The RAM heap allows:
1. Object creation
2. Reading of object fields
3. Update of object fields

As a reflection of the longer word size of the disk, the operations on the disk heap are modified to:
1. Object creation
2. Reading whole objects
3. Updating whole objects

There are three additional operations in PS-algol disk heaps:

4. Start a transaction
5. Abort a transaction
6. Commit a transaction

These operations are a reflection of the non-volatility of the heap. They will be familiar to database implementors, but perhaps less familiar to programming language people. An atomic transaction is a transformation of a database from one consistent state to another. Clearly in carrying this out we may have to go through intermediate states that are not themselves consistent. But these intermediate states must not be visible from outside the transaction. From the outside it must look as if the transaction occurred in an instant, in a single quantum of time.

Time on computers is quantized. To the hardware designer the quantum is the clock cycle. To the compiler writer it is the machine instruction. To the database implementor it is the time taken for a single disk access. The requirement of a database transaction is that the disk image of the database should evolve by a series of quantum steps between internally consistent states. And it should do this irrespective of possible hardware and software errors.

Suppose we have a simple model of persistence in which objects are sent back to disk at the end of a program. What will happen if we get an error of some sort as the objects are in train of passage to disk?

You could have some of the data written back with new values whilst other parts of the disk still held the old values when the crash occurred. The resulting mix of old and new state information might well be contradictory. In a screen editor it is conventional to get round this by copying the old state of a file to a backup file before the new version is saved. You can then go back to the previous version if you have made a mistake. PS-algol differs from an editor in that it uses incremental transfers of data between store layers. In these circumstances, where only a small portion of the database may be changed by a program, taking a complete backup copy would be excessive.

As PS-algol implementations have evolved, different techniques have been adopted to handle this problem. Two of them, the POMS and the CPOMS will be described in detail.

The POMS, which stood for Persistent Object Management System, was developed in 1983. It was a complete PS-algol storage manger implemented recursively in PS-algol itself. Its approach to providing secure transactions was to use a technique termed shadow paging. When data was written back to disk during a transaction it was written to different site from where it had originated. This meant that no data which was valid at the start of the transaction was

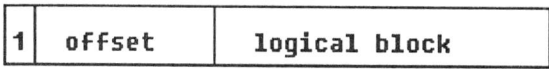

Figure 8.1 PID mark II

modified prior to the transaction committing. If the transaction aborted the previous consistent state was still there on disk. This technique exploits the fact that disk transfers occur in long words, usually refered to as disk blocks. An address on disk can be thought of as having two components:

i) the block number
ii) the offset into the block

POMS distinguished between *logical* blocks and *relative* blocks. A relative block occupied a fixed position within a file and was identified by a *relative block number*. A logical block was characterized by a *logical block number* and could occupy different relative blocks at different times. A table was provided, termed the *LR.map* which mapped logical block numbers to relative block numbers such that, if L is a logical number, then $LR.map(L)$ was the corresponding relative block number.

The Persistent ID used in the POMS could, at first approximation be thought of as looking like Figure 8.1. Objects on disk were addressed in terms of their logical block and an offset from the start of the block.

Every transaction that modified a block caused it to be written back to a different relative block. The *LR.map* held the currently valid mapping between logical and relative blocks within the database.

In order to provide a secure commit to a transaction the following algorithm was executed:

1. Determine which items on the RAM heap have been modified in the course of the transaction.

2. Assign a new relative block to each logical block containing modified items, and write the block containing the updated items back to disk.

3. Update the *LR.map* and send it back to disk.

Any failure in the first two phases left an unmodified *LR.map* on the disk. In consequence the next transaction to come along sees the database as being unmodified. The *LR.map* created two types of address space on disk:

relative and logical. Of these, the second had the vital property of being transactionally secure. Changes in the state of the logical address space were atomic provided that the update of the *LR.map* was itself atomic.

8.1 IMPLEMENTATION OF THE *LR.MAP*

In principle the *LR.map* was just a big array acting as a lookup table. In practice this approach was subtly modified. POMS allowed 2^{15} logical blocks in a database. If a single vector of this size was used to implement the map, then small databases would have an unacceptably high overhead. In addition there would have been the risk that a hardware failure might have occurred whilst the *LR.map* was being written to disk. This would have resulted in a corrupt database.

The problem was solved by dividing the *LR.map* into two parts, one fixed and one extendible. The fixed part was small enough to hold a single disk block. This held the LR mapping of the first n blocks of the logical address space. The expansible part then held the mapping for the blocks in the range n to *max.blocks.*.

PS-algol implements arrays as Iliffe vectors, that is to say an n dimensional array is implemented as an array of pointers to $n-1$ dimensional arrays. This technique was used to implement the extendible part as a partially populated array of integers.

    let LR.map = **vector** 1::8 **of**
        vector 0::lr.lev.size **of**
        vector 0::lr.lev.sixe **of** 0

The constant *lr.lev.size* was tailored to allow at least one of the vectors to fit into a disk block.

8.1.1 Recursive implementation of LR map in logical space

One important consequence of implementing the LR map in two parts was that the extensible part could exist in the *logical* disk address space. This followed inevitably from the decision to represent the *LR.map* as a PS-algol array. On disk PS-algol objects have their pointers implemented as PIDs. PIDs define points in logical disk address space. Thus a PS-algol array must exist in logical address space. But it was also a requirement that the system exist in logical address space if transactions were to be safe.

All state changes to the logical address space were implemented as atomic transactions. If the *LR.map* extension is placed in logical rather than relative address space then all changes to its state become atomic transactions as well. This argument is obviously circular. Whether the circle is virtuous or vicious depends upon whether a fixed point can be defined. The fixed point was the fixed portion of the *LR.map*.

This all fitted in a single disk block. If we assume that the output of a single block to disk is a transaction in hardware terms, that made changes to the fixed portion of the the *LR.map* transactionally secure. The trick was to make the transactional properties of the rest of the *LR.map* depend upon those of the fixed part.

For this to happen the following condition had to be true:

If an object A is itself part of the mapping system, the lowest logical block number in whose mapping it participates must be higher than the logical block number of A itself.

Adherence to this will ensure the stability of the whole mapping system and thus of the store itself.

It turns out that if the fixed part of the map is capable of holding the logical to relative mappings of the first 3 blocks of the relative address space that is enough. The extensible portion of the map is a 3 dimensional array. As shown

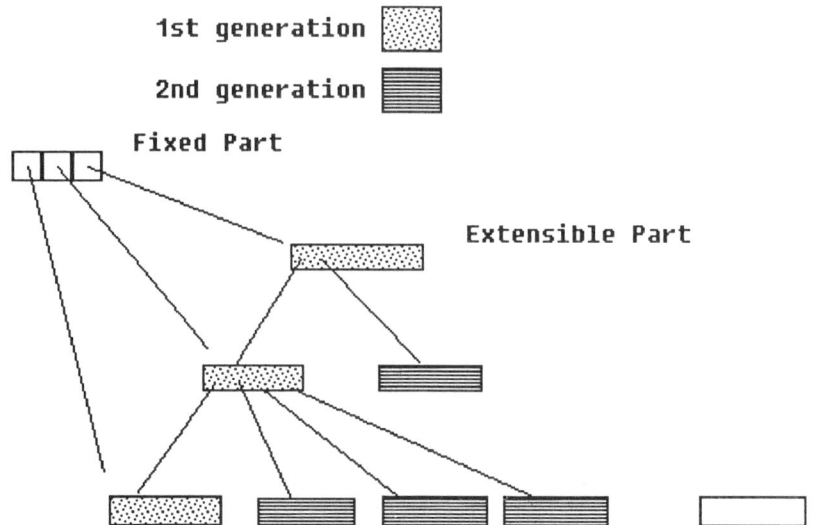

Figure 8.2 The fixed portion of the LR.map maps the first generation of the expansible portion.

in Figure 8.2, the fixed portion of the map specified the relative addresses on disk of the shaded portion of the extensible portion. This we term the first generation of the *LR.map*. The first generation comprises the set { *LR.map, LR.map(1), LR.map(1,0)* }. This will itself specify the mapping of a further *(lr.lev.size +1)* blocks. These comprise the second generation. In the figure we assume *lr.lev.size =3* . This means that the second generation contains the nodes *LR.map(1,1)* to *LR.map(1,3)* and also the node *LR.map(2)* . The leaf nodes of the second generation, will specify a further *lr.lev.size x (lr.lev.size +1)* mappings. Not all of these will be used for mapping the mappings. The number of mappings grows rapidly and the surplus ones are used to map other objects.

8.2 CLASS FRACTIONS

Disk store is much slower than RAM. If you are using disk it is wise to minimize the number of disk transfers that take place. Since a disk read is capable of bringing in several objects at a time, it is desirable to bring in several objects that you are likely to need. A common activity is following linked lists or traversing trees. In RAM it makes no difference to the speed of your program where in the address space the elements of the list are placed. On disk it makes a big difference.

In the design of the disk placement algorithms for POMS it was assumed that access to linked lists would be common. An attempt was made to put items that were likely to be on the same list next to one another on disk. It was assumed that a list is likely to be made up of items of a single structure class. PIDs were allocated to structures using these rules:

> a) Items of a given class were gathered together into sets of blocks which were termed the fractions of the class.
> b) Each logical block contained members of only one class.
> c) When allocating PIDs to a linked list, try to put adjacent list items into the same logical block.

For every class in the database there was a class descriptor. This held information common to the class as a whole. This included a list of free pids available for storage of class members, and a use list of the class fractions that contained objects from this class. The class descriptors were accessed via a table indexed on the class identifiers.

The class fraction mechanism was also extended to handle strings and vectors. Such objects do not fall into classes but they can still be grouped according to size so that objects of the same size could be clustered together into a disk block. For strings and vectors there is more variation in sizes than there is with structures; this could lead to a proliferation of disk blocks containing single items - the only 43 character string in the database for instance. As a compromise non **pntr** objects were grouped together on a logarithmic scale. Each object was assigned a class fraction that depended upon the $\log_2$ of their size. Thus there would be logical blocks for objects containing 2:3 words, 4:7 words, 8:15 words etc.

8.3 PROBLEMS WITH THE POMS

What has been presented above is only part of the features of the Persistent Object Management System. A full description is contained in the article *Persistent Object Management System*, in the January 1984 edition of *Software Practice and Experience*. The POMS was an elegant solution to the problem of disk organization. It was implemented in the language that it supported: PS-algol. This aided its portability. The PS-algol system on most machines was interpretive. To get it working on a machine, you wrote an interpreter for the abstract machine code along with a garbage collector. The whole of the persistence management system then ported directly since it was pure PS-algol. However, in 1984 an extension was made to the syntax of PS-algol to allow the use of procedure variables. Procedures became first class citizens. This involved changes to the abstract machine that led to a considerable degradation in performance. Since the persistence management system was itself implemented in PS-algol, any degradation in basic machine performance produced a squared degradation in overall system performance.

A choice had to be made, either we gave up the idea of using first class functions, or we had to implement a faster system of disk store management. What was done was to reimplement the POMS in C. The new software was called the CPOMS.

8.4 CPOMS

The format of a PID was altered in the CPOMS. The new format is shown in Figure 8.3.

The PID is made up as before of a sign bit that is set to distinguish it from a machine address, and then 2 fields. The first is a 15 bit partition number and the second is a 16 bit object number. The partitions are logical subdivisions of the address space. The databases that the PS-algol programmer sees will be made up of one or more partitions. The assignment of partitions to databases is

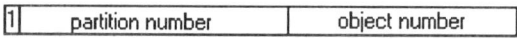

Figure 8.3 A CPOMS PID

recorded in the partitions file. This is an array with 2^{15} short integers that maps partitions to database numbers.

Associated with each partition there is a datafile, that contains all of the objects in the partition. The collection of partition files is held in a single directory on the Unix system.

Databases themselves are comprised of:
i) a set of partitions
ii) a count of the locks held on the database
iii) an owner number
iv) a name
v) a password
vi) an index file.

The database lock count can either be -1 to indicate that it is locked for writing, 0 to indicate that it is free or > 0 to indicate the number of processes that have locked the database for reading. The owner number is taken from the Unix operating system and is simply the system User ID. The name and password serve to identify the database and to control access. The information about directories is stored in a file called the database directory. This is essentially a

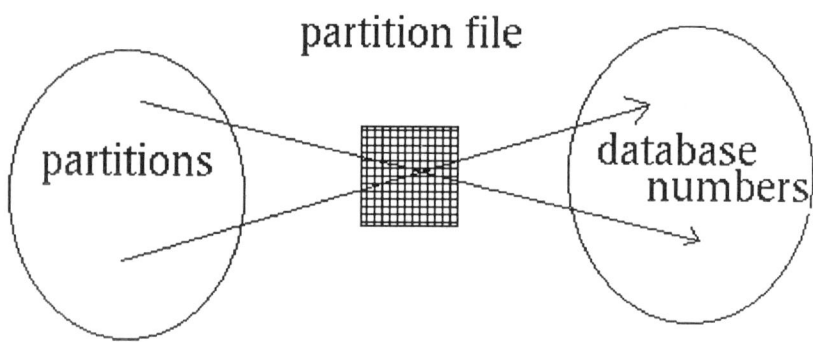

Figure 8.4 The partition file

vector of database structures.

The index file is used to translate object numbers to offsets in the relevant partition data file. Assume we have a vector of datafiles then we can view the logical mapping from PID to disk address as the composition of maps thus

disk.address(partition,object) =
  datafile(partition)(
    database.directory(partitionfile(partition))(indexfile)(object)
)

This mapping could be carried out directly by reading the files concerned but the number of disk accesses per object fetched would be excessive. To speed it up a cache is maintained called the PTODI or Partition to Database and Index map. This is a PS-algol vectors that holds triples of the form

[partition, database, index]

The vector is scanned until the partition that is being looked for is found. The next two entries in the vector then specify a database number and an offset into an index file. The process is shown in Figure 8.5.

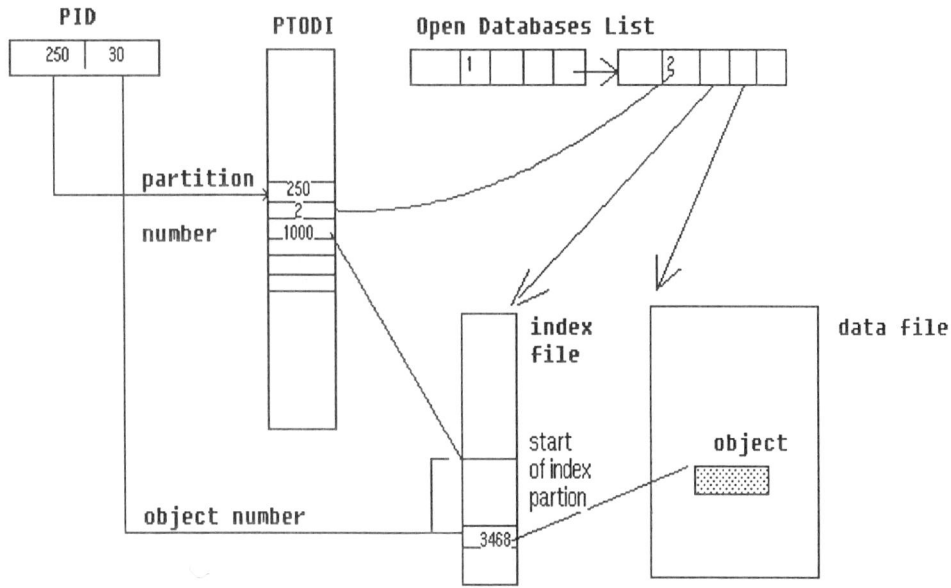

Figure 8.5 The use of the PTODI map

We start off trying to index PID [250,30]. The PTODI is searched using 250 as a key. This returns us [2,1000]. The first number, 2, tells us which of the open databases contains this partition. Using this we obtain the file descriptors of the index file and the data file for this database. The second number, 1000, tells us at what offset into the index file information about this partition is held. Adding this to the offset field of the PID we obtain 1030 as the entry in the index file to be consulted. At location 1030 in the index file we find the value 3468 which is the offset into the data file at which the object is to be found. The object can then be read into the volatile heap.

At commit time, the same mapping process can be used to locate where objects are to be placed on disk when they are written back to the database.

9

First Class Functions and Modular Compilation

Suppose you want to construct a library of procedures that perform numeric conversions. We might for example define functions to map integers and reals to strings:

```
let int.format = proc(int i ->string)
begin
    let sign= if i<0 then "-" else ""
    let zero = decode ("0")
    if i<0 do i:= -i
    let s:=code( zero +(i rem 10))
    repeat
    {
        i:= i div 10
    }
    while i >0 do s:= code(zero +( i rem 10 )) ++ s
        sign ++s
end
```

```
let pad = proc(string s; int width->string)
         begin
                ! code to pad a string out with leading spaces
         end
let fp.format= proc(real n;int w,d->string)
begin
    ! floating point conversion
    ! w digits before decimal point
    ! d digits after + exponent
    ! calls pad

end
```

Example 9.1

We could include these in every program that was being written, but that would slow down compilation unjustifiably. What we want to do is compile them once and then have them callable by more than one other program. Two different approaches have been taken in the S-algol class of languages to deal with this problem.

9.1 SALGOL

In the original S-algol the approach was conventional and very similar to what one would do in languages like FORTRAN or C. It involved the three stage process shown in Figure 9.1. First the library was compiled using the **ext** compiler extension. Hence one might type:

sc convlib.S ext

Where the **ext** option was used to tell the compiler that this was a file just containing external procedures. The file was restricted to containing procedure declarations. In the S-algol syntax the code would look likeExample 9.2.

When compiling in the ext mode, there are restrictions on the scope rules of the language. Procedures are normally represented at run time in S-algol by closures on the stack. When a procedure is declared, a couple of words on the stack are reserved to hold the procedures address. A call is to the procedure then made via the closure. An external library is never executed as a program so there is no opportunity to push closures corresponding to procedures onto the stack. In consequence the normal scope rules that allow a procedure that allow procedures to call one another will not work. The procedure int.format in

```
! Maths conversion library convlib.s
procedure int.format(int i ->string)
begin
    let sign= if i<0 then "-" else ""
    let zero = decode ("0")
    if i<0 do i:= -i
    let s:=code( zero +(i rem 10))
    repeat
    {      i:= i div 10  }
    while i >0 do s:= code(zero +( i rem 10 )) ++ s
        sign ++s
end
procedure pad (string s;  int width->string)
        begin
              ! code to pad a string out with leading spaces
        end
procedure fp.format(real n;int w,d->string)
begin
    ! floating point conversion
    ! w digits before decimal point
    ! d digits after  + exponent
    ! calls pad
end
```
Example 9.2

the example above will not be able to see the procedure pad. Instead, what we have to do is provide some mechanism by which procedures can be called by name. This was done using the **external** declaration. For instance to allow fp.format to call pad we would write:

```
procedure fp.format(real n;int w,d->string)
begin
    ! floating point conversion
    ! w digits before decimal point
    ! d digits after  + exponent
    ! calls pad
      external  pad (string , int ->string)
    ! code to do the actual conversion
end
```

When fp.format was run then the **external** declaration of pad would cause a closure for pad to be pushed onto the stack making it callable inside fp.format. Similarly, any program that wanted to use these procedures would have to declare them as externals:

! program writeint.s
external int.format(**int -> string**)
write int.format(8)
?

For a procedure to be callable it is obviously necessary for it to be present in RAM at run time. S-algol does this using what it terms a binder which is like what other languages call a linker. Suppose we have compiled **convlib.s** to **convlib.out** as shown above. We then compile and bind our program:

sc writeint.s
sb writeint.out convlib.out =writei.out

The binder program **sb** merges the two files **writeint.out** and **convlib.out** to form a new file **writei.out**. The **external** procedure declarations have been replaced by instructions to form closures for the bound procedures.

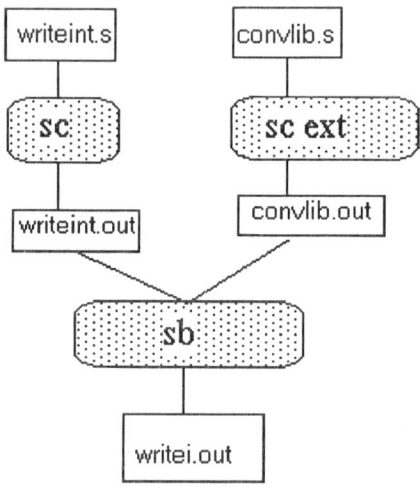

Figure 9.1 S-algol external linkage

```
let int.format = proc(int i ->string)
begin
    let sign= if i<0 then "-" else ""
    let zero = decode ("0")
    if i<0 do i:= -i
    let s:=code( zero +(i rem 10))
    repeat
    {
        i:= i div 10
    }
    while i >0 do s:= code(zero +( i rem 10 )) ++ s
            sign ++
end
let pad = proc(string s;  int width->string)
        begin
                ! code to pad a string out with leading spaces
        end
let fp.format= proc(real n;int w,d->string)
begin
    ! floating point conversion
    ! w digits before decimal point
    ! d digits after + exponent
    ! calls pad
end
structure conv.pack(
        proc(int->string)i.format;
        proc(real,int,int,->string)f.format
)
let p = conv.pack(int.format,fp.format)
let lib = create.database("conv.lib", "", "write")
s.enter("math.conv",lib,p)
if commit( ) do write "library initialized"
?
```
        Example 9.3

The binder differs from a conventional Fortran or C linker in that it performs type checking on externals.

9.2 PS-ALGOL

The separate compilation facilities in PS-algol derive from its use of first class functions. By first class functions we mean that functions or procedures acquire the same 'civil rights' as other types.

Whatever you can do with any type other than a function can be done with a function itself. Given type **t** in PS-algol you can declare a variable of type **t**, or a constant of type **ct**. If you have a variable, values of type **t** can be assigned to it. You can create a vector of type ***t** and you can create functions of type **proc**(anything ->t) or **proc**(t ->anything). With PS-algol the same applies to functions.

Functions became data values just like any other and could be stored in structures, variables and vectors. These structures are then themselves stored on the persistent heap. In the previous example we would write a program that stores all the conversion procedures in a database.

This has placed the structure **p** which contains the two procedures that we wish to keep in the database **conv.lib**. In a language like C what would have been stored in **p** would have been the RAM address of the function. For Algol-like languages this is not good enough. A procedure needs to have access to its context of declaration, so procedure values are represented by closures, which are pairs made up of a code pointer and a static link. The code pointer points at the instructions and the static link points at the context of declaration. In the early versions of PS-algol, this static link just pointed into the stack as described in Chapter 6, but when first class functions were introduced this mechanism became inadequate.

The S-algol closures were made up of two RAM addresses, one pointing to code, the other being an offset into the stack. If we tried to implement Example 9.2 that way what would happen?

A pair of RAM addresses representing **fp.format** would be stored in the structure which in its turn would go out to disk. But what would the addresses refer to once stored on disk? They originally referred to the positions in memory of the code and stack. Following standard PS-algol techniques these should be turned into PIDs, but PIDs to what?

The question of how to represent the code pointer in the persistent store is not too difficult. The compiler just has to be modified so that the binary code for each procedure is preceded by an appropriate heap object header. The

POMS or CPOMS will then automatically transfer the code to disk. The static link part of the closure for the procedure **fp.format** will point at the lowest stack frame, the one that holds the global variables. The arrangement is shown in Figure 9.2.

Procedure **fp.format** may need to have access to global variables when it is called. In the example it will need to get at the closure of **pad**. Normally this would have been stored on the main stack. After the program has committed, the stack would have disappeared since it is not formatted as a heap object capable of being saved by the commit algorithm. In consequence the next time the procedure is called, after it had been retrieved from the database, it would have lost the environment in which it was declared. It would no longer be able to access any of the old global variables. To get round this it is necessary to so construct the stack that it too could be saved in the database on a commit. The stack is packaged up in a stack frame object that can be transferred to and from disk. Into this object must go both the stacks, pointer and main. In front of it must go a heap header. We end up with the arrangements shown in Figure 9.3.

The pointer and main stacks are packed into a single object and grow in opposite directions towards each other. Procedure closures are now made up of two components [code object pointer, stack frame object pointer]. As pointers they must now reside on the P stack.

The invention of the stack frame object allows procedures to be stored

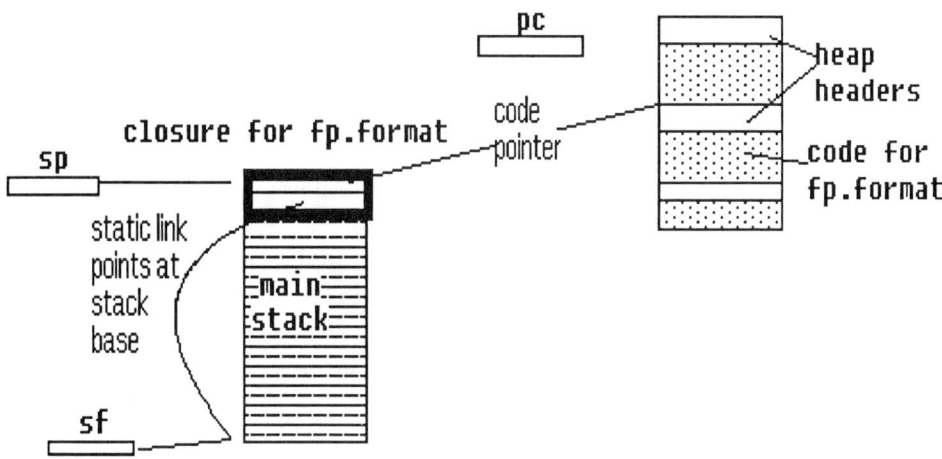

Figure 9.2 A initial step towards first class procedures.

in the database. It also allows procedures to be returned by other procedures. Consider Example 9.4.

```
let make.counter= proc(->proc(->int))
begin
    let tally :=0
    let counter = proc(->int)
    begin
            tally:=tally+1
            tally
    end
    ! now return counter as the result of make.counter
    counter
end
let counter.1 = make.counter()
let counter.2 = make.counter()
write counter.1(),counter.1(), counter.2(),counter.1()

>    1    2    1    3
```

Example 9.4

The procedure **make.counter** can be called at any time to create a new counter procedure. Each of these counter procedures returns 1 the first time it is called and delivers successive integers on subsequent invocations. Each counter procedure has access to a distinct copy of the variable **tally** that was initialized to zero for it when **make.counter** was called.

It is not possible to implement this semantics using a traditional stack based system of variable allocation. If a stack was used to create space for **tally** then the location would have been released when control returned from **make.counter.** The counter procedures would end up associating the variable **tally** with a stack address that was likely to be corrupted by subsequent procedure calls.

This problem can be overcome if we create a new stack object for each procedure invocation. When **make.counter** is called, a new stack object is created on the heap, containing within itself a small P stack and a little M stack. Zero is pushed onto the little M stack to represent **tally** and a closure is formed

Ch.9] FIRST CLASS FUNCTIONS 111

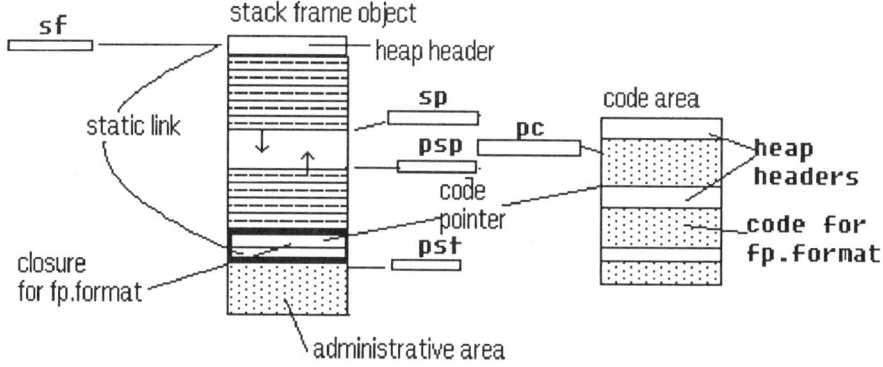

Figure 9.3. A PS-algol stack frame object

on the P stack to represent **counter**. The static link of this closure points at the stack object and the code pointer refers to the instructions for counter.

The stacks within the stack object are used both to store variables and for expression evaluation. Each stack object has an administrative area in which registers can be cached when a nested procedure call is made. The administrative area also contains a display pointing at the stack objects of lexically enclosing procedures. The display allows access to intermediate variables.

The standard PS-algol method of procedure call and storage allocation

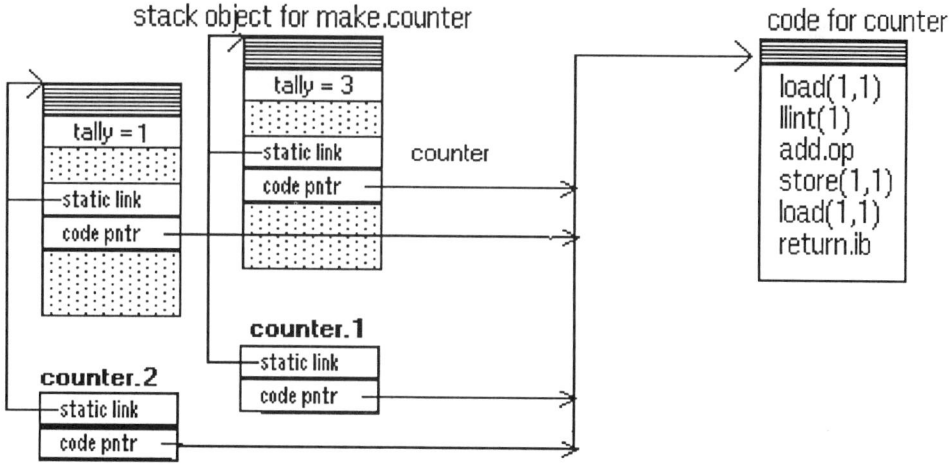

Figure 9.4 Data created by example 9.4

112   FIRST CLASS FUNCTIONS   [Ch.9]

is inefficient. In the great majority of calls there is no real need to create a stack object on the heap, since most procedures do not return other procedures. Only those that do, really need to have a frame allocated for them on the heap. Stack allocation and release is much more efficient than heap allocation. With a stack, store can be recovered simply using the return instruction. Heap store has to be de-allocated by the garbage collector which takes a lot longer. In code that

```
! program writeint.S PS-algol version
! open the database that contains the package
let lib = open.database("convlib","", "read")
if lib is error.record do begin
        write "open database failed"
        abort
end
! use a table lookup function to extract the package
let pack = s.lookup("math.conv",lib)
if s = nil do begin
        write "math.conv pack not found "
        abort
end
! put int a declaration of what we expect the package to look like
structure conv.pack(
        proc(int->string)i.format;
        proc(real,int,int,->string)f.format
)
! extract the procedure we want
let int.format = pack(i.format)
write int.format(8)
?
```

Example 9.5

makes many procedure calls, garbage collection can take up a large portion of the run time.

A more intelligent compiler should be able to identify which variables need to be given space on the heap and which can safely be left on the stack. The stack can be used for:

a) Variables in procedures that contain no nested procedure.

b) Variables in procedures which, although they do contain nested procedures, do not contain any nested procedures that are passed outwith their context of declaration.

c) Variables that are not referred to by nested procedures that are passed outwith their context of declaration.

The only remaining variables are those that are referred to by procedures that pass outwith their context of declaration. These do need to be allocated on the heap. A two pass compiler can classify variables according to these rules into those that could be allocated on the stack in the normal way and those that need heap store. This optimization has been tried on some experimental compilers but it is not used in any of the standard releases.

9.3 DYNAMIC LINKING

Because procedures are values living in the persistent store, a distinct linkage phase is not necessary to gain access to separately compiled code. To use the numeric conversion procedures they would have to be fetched back from the database, so that in PS the program **writeint.S** would look like Example 9.5.

The PS-algol mechanism was an improvement on the S-algol mechanism in two respects. It allows library procedures access to 'hidden' variables, what were called 'own' variables in algol-60 or 'static' variables in C. Secondly it is dynamic, a program can decide which procedures it wants to use. Suppose that several different versions of a procedure are stored in the database: for instance different device drivers. A program can chose at run time which one it wants to be linked to. The main disadvantage of the PS-algol mechanism, besides its slowness, is that it leaves a lot of work to the programmer. It is verbose. The programmer has to write additional code to put the procedures into and fetch the procedures from the database.

9.4 PERSISTENT S-ALGOL LINKAGE

Persistent S-algol does not support first class functions and its linkage mechanism is based upon an extension to that used in the S-algol system.

The compiler recognizes that a collection of procedures is to be compiled as a library by the presence of the **segment** directive on the first line of the program. This instructs the compiler that the procedures that follow are to be compiled into a library segment. Hence our example would be like the S-algol one but with a new heading:

>   **segment** "convlib"
>   procedure int.format .....
>   procedure pad .....
>   procedure fp.format .....

As with S-algol this is compiled to produce a file **convlib.out.** The difference comes in the binding mechanism. In Persistent S-algol this is dynamic. If at run time the declaration of an external is encountered, a call is made upon the dynamic binder to find the external procedure.

The external declarations now look like:

>   ! program writeint Persistent S-algol version
>   **let** i.format = **import** ("int.format")(**int   ->string**) **segment** "conv.lib"
>   **write** i.format(8)

This mechanism is relatively concise compared with the PS-algol mechanism shown previously. Yet it retains many of the advantages. The mechanism is dynamic. The name of the procedure and the segment from which it is to be found are strings. They could be determined at run time. Consider the following example:

let display = **import** ("display.type") (**->string**) **segment** "graphics"
! display returns the name of the display type "cga","ega" etc
let draw = **import** (display()++"draw") (**int ,int,int,int**) **segment** "graphics"

How is this implemented?

The compiler translates the **import** clause into code to push three strings onto the stack:
1. The external name of the procedure
2. The type of the procedure
3. The segment from which it is to be found

The compiler then plants a call to the run time binder which is a

```
org 100h
        jmp p1
        ....
p1:     jmp p2
        dw  10
        db 'int.format'
        dw 22
        db 'procedure(int->string)'
        enter 0,0
        push i
        ....
        retf
p2      jmp p3
        dw 3
        db 'pad'
        dw 29
        db 'procedure(string,int->string)'
        enter 0,0
        ....
p3      jmp p4
....
p4      mov ax,4c00h
        int 21h; program terminate
```

Example 9.6

procedure of the form:
    bind(string pname, ptyrpe, segname -> procedure.address)

The result of the call to bind is a closure on the stack just as in a normal procedure declaration. From then on the imported procedure, under its new name can be used like any other.

The binder could work in a number of ways, it might fetch the segment in from persistent store, or it might fetch it in from the filing system. Currently the procedure looks in the file directory defined by the environment variable **PSDIR** for a file of the same name as the segment but with a **.out** suffix. It then calls upon the heap manager to allocate a segment for the file and loads it into memory. The binder maintains a segment table that maps the names of resident segments to their store addresses.

Having found a segment the binder has to find the procedures in the segment. Since this is a library segment it does not have to do anything, but we do not want it to cause any problems if someone inadvertently executes it. The answer to both these requirements it for the library segment to consist of a jump chain as shown in Example 9.6.

Should the library segment be inadvertently executed, it simply performs a series of jumps that take it to the program terminate system call. The linker uses the same jump chain to locate the procedure headers. These consist of the names and types of the procedures, formatted as S-algol strings: a length word followed by the characters.

9.4.1 Dynamic linkage to alien procedures

The dynamic linker is also used to allow Persistent S-algol programs to call procedures written in C or assembler. These arise in two contexts:

    a) invisible procedures that the compiler invokes

    b) **alien** procedures that are explicitly declared

Invisible procedures are invoked by the compiler when one of the built-in operations of the language is too complex to perform with in line code. Obvious examples are floating point arithmetic and input/output. Less obvious examples are operations which access data in the virtual memory. Consider a vector assignment operation:

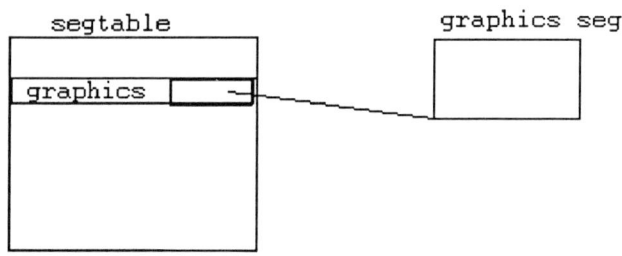

Figure 9.5 Use of the resident segment table in Persistent S-algol

x(5) := 9

This will be performed by calling a C procedure

subvassi(bx,val,index,vector)
int bx,val,index;PID vector;

so the S-algol statement is equivalent to a C call

subvassi(bx,9,5,x)

Note that the parameters are pushed onto the stack in reverse order in C on an Intel type machine since the stack grows downwards. In machines where the stack grows upwards, the parameters would be pushed in the normal order. This is the case on the Linn Rekursiv implementation for example.

This C call will translate into:

```
lea si,[x+bx]           ;bx is global base register
add sp,-ptrstackbytes   ; create space on stack
mov di,ss               ; make es point at stack
mov es,di
mov di,sp               ; set destination register
mov cx,ptrstacklen      ; length of a pointer
rep movsw               ; block move instruction
push 5                  ; vector index
push 9                  ; value to be assigned
push bx                 ; bx may be altered by C code
int 18h                 ; call level 1 dynamic binder
db '_subvassi',0        ; procedure called
pop bx                  ; restore the bx register
add sp, 20              ; remove params from stack as per C convention
```

Example 9.7.

The call is done via software interrupt followed by a C string giving the procedure name. The interrupt transfers control to the binder. The binder is part of the programs **psr** and **s**. It is provided with a pair of arrays declared in the file **procdef.c**. These associate the names of files with their addresses. The file is

shown in abbreviated form in Example 9.8.
/*
   S-ALGOL dynamic linker driver table
           this contains two arrays used by the dynamic linker
        proctable : this contains the addresses of all
               the C and assembler routines called
               by S-algol
        PROCNAME : this contains the names by which these
               C routines will be called from within
               S-algol

to make a C procedure callable from S-algol carry out
the following steps:
1. write your C procedure
    suppose you have a procedure called 'bazonka'
  in a file bazonka.c
    bazonka(struct saframe pad ,int a,int b)
       {
       }
       where an saframe is given by
#define SAFRAME 5
struct saframe{ short padding[SAFRAME] ; };

2. Compile it with Turbo C
     tcc -mh -c bazonka

  3. Include this in the S-algol libraries
       tlib salibf.lib +-bazonka.obj
       tlib salibh.lib +-bazonka.obj

  4. Edit this file so that the new first entry in proctable is
       (int*) bazonka,

   and the first entry in PROCNAME is
       {"_bazonka"}

  5. Compile this file and add it to the S-algol libraries

```
        tcc -mh -c procdef
         tlib salibf.lib +-procdef.obj
       tlib salibh.lib +-procdef.obj
```

6. Recompile the compiler driver and run time driver files
   ```
   tcc -mh -M s.obj salibf.lib 7layerh.lib
   tcc -mh -M psr.obj salibf.lib  7layerh.lib
   ```

7. Declare the c routine in your S-algol program
            procedure bazonka(int b,a); alien ''_bazonka''

```
*/
#include "link.h"
#define MAXPROC 92
int maxproc = MAXPROC;
int  ARGC(),
ARGV(),
 clearscreen(),
..........,
..........,
 TAN(),
 ATAN(),
 TRUNCATE(),
 FLOAT_LOWER(),
 FLOAT_TOP(),
 Returncode(), /* called by compiler to obtain the line a program
                         terminated on in the event of error */
 TERMINATE(),
 bind(),
 saerror();

int far *proctable [MAXPROC]={
 (int*) ARGC,
 (int*)ARGV,
 (int*)clearscreen,
........,
..........,(int*)
```

```
    TAN,(int* )
    ATAN,(int* )
    TRUNCATE,(int* )
    FLOAT_LOWER,(int* )
    FLOAT_TOP,(int* )
    Returncode,
    (int*)TERMINATE,
    (int*)bind,
    /* padding */
    (int*)saerror
    } ;

#define install(a) {a}

struct identifier PROCNAME[MAXPROC] ={
install(''_ARGC''),
install(''_ARGV''),
install(''_clearscreen''),
........,
........,
install(''_TAN''),
install(''_ATAN''),
install(''_TRUNCATE''),
install(''_float_lower''),
install(''_float_top''),
install(''Returncode''),
install(''_terminate''),
install(''_bind''),    /* the level2 dynamic binder */
install(''_saerror'')
};
```
Example 9.8

This file is statically linked to the C and assembly language routines that make up the run time program **psr**. When an interrupt 18h is invoked, the binder searches PROCNAME to find the routine whose name follows the interrupt. It obtains the name from the interrupt return address which will be pointing at the first character of the name. Once it has found the routines name in PROCNAME it overwrites the interrupt instruction with a call. It then overwrites the first 4 characters of the procedure name with the procedures address that it has found and overwrites any remaining letters of the procedure name with NOP instructions. It then subtracts 2 from the interrupt return address on the stack so that it points back at the start of the old interrupt instruction, (which is now the call instruction) and does a return from interrupt.

On return the first thing the S-algol program does is to re-try the call which now takes it directly where it wanted to go. On all subsequent occasions the call will be taken directly.

This level one dynamic binder can also be invoked for explicitly declared procedures that are implemented in low level languages. For example the assembler routines that enable access to the Microsoft mouse bios are declared as:

! Microsoft MOUSE BIOS
let mouse.x = **proc(->int)**; **alien** ''_mousex''
! x position of the mouse

let mouse.y = **proc(->int)**;**alien** ''_mousey''
! y position of the mouse

let mouse.buttons = **proc(->int)**;**alien** ''_mousebut''
! returns bit to indicate if mouse buttons down

These are re-labled calls on a set of C routines. For instance ''mouse.buttons'' calls :

```
Smousebut(struct saframe pad,int x)
{ x = MOUSEBUT();}
```

Which in turn calls the assembler routine:

```
_MOUSEBUT PROC far
          mov ax,3
          int 33h
          mov ax,bx
          ret
_MOUSEBUT ENDP
```

Note the differences in the differences in the procedure result mechanisms of C and S-algol. S-algol expects the procedure result on the stack, C expects it in the ax register, and the mouse bios returns it in the bx register.

So what happens when an S-algol program calls the mouse.buttons procedure?

Suppose we have the statement

b := mouse.buttons()

this will translate into:

```
add sp,2         ; space for result
call far pntr [bx + mouse.buttons]
pop [bx + b]     ; perform assignment
```

This is an indirect call using a procedure address on the stack. The S-algol mouse buttons procedure itself will just be a stub that uses the dynamic linker to call the C routine.

```
enter 0,1
push bx
int 18h
db '_mousebut',0
pop bx
ret
```

The use of this indirect call mechanism means that the parameters or return address of the procedure have had the return address of the S-algol mouse.buttons procedure and the bx register pushed on top of them. The space these will occupy is declared in C using the "pad" variable of type saframe.

The use of dynamic linking in Persistent S-algol allows many of the late binding features of PS-algol first class functions to be implemented without the relatively high memory and heap overhead involved with block retention. Once the linker has been invoked the first time, further calls proceed as fast as statically linked code would. The combination of these two techniques allows Persistent S-algol to be implemented on personal computers of relatively modest performance, which was one of the original motivations for the development of S-algol.

Bibliography

Software

MSDOS version is available from the Department of Computer Science, University of Strathclyde, Glasgow, Scotland, price £49 for binary version. It is supplied on an IBM PC AT disk. It is an integrated package which includes a menu driven editor and interactive compiler. The user interface and performance is comparable to leading commercial compilers for the IBM PC. It supports graphics for the VGA and EGA displays. Cheques should be made out to the University of Strathclyde.

Books

Davie, A J T & Morrison, R. "Recursive Descent Compiling", Ellis Horwood Press (1981)

Atkinson, M P (ed). "Databases". Pergammon Infotech State of the Art Reports, Serioes 9, No.8, January 1982 (535 pages)

Cole, A J & Morrison, R. "An Introduction to programming with S-Algol". Cambridge University Press, Cambridge, 1982

Stocker, P M., Atkinson, M P., & Grey, P M D (eds) "Databases - Roll and Structure". Cambridge University Press, Cambridge, 1984.

Published Papers

Morrison R, "A method of implementing procedure entry and exit in block structured high level languages". Software, Practical and Experience 7, 5 (July 1977), 535-537

Morrison R, & Podolski, Z. "The Graffiti graphics system". Proc. of the DECUS Conference, Bath (April 1978), 5-10

Gunnm H I E & Morrison, R. "On the implementation of constants", Information Processing Letters 9, 1 (July 1979), 1-4.

Atkinson, M.P. "Data management for interactive graphics". Proceeding of the Infotech State of the ARt Conference, October 1979. Available as EUCs departmental report CSR-51-80.

Atkinson, M P (ed). "Data Design". Infotech State of the Art Report, Series 7, No.4. May 1980.

Morrison, R. "Low cost computer graphics for micro computers". Software Practice and Experience, 12, 1981, 767-776.

BIBLIOGRAPHY

Atkinson, M P., Chisholm, K J & Cockshott, W P, "PS-algol: An Algol with a Persistent Heap". ACM SIGPLAN Notices Vol. 17, No.7. (July 1981) 24-31. Also as EUCS Departmental Report CSR-94-81.

Atkinson, M P., Chisholm, K J., & Cockshott, W P. "Nepal - the New Edinburgh Persistent Algorithimic Language". Database, Pergammon Infotech State of the Art Report, Series 9, No.8. 299-318 (January 1982) - also as EUCS Departmental Report CSR-90-81.

Morrison, R. "S-algol: a simple algol". Computer Bulletin II/31 (March 1982).

Morrison, R. "The string as a simple data type". Sigplan Notices, Vol.17,3, 46-52, 1982.

Atkinson, M.P., Bailey, P J., Chisholm, K J., Cockshott, W P & Morrison, R. "Progress with Persistent Programming" presented at CREST course UEA, September 1982, revised in "Databases - Role and Structure". see PERSISTENT PROGRAMMING RESEARCH REPORTR-8-84.

Morrison, R. "Towards simpler programming langauges: S-algol" IUCC Bulletin 4, 3 (October 1982), 130-133.

Atkinson, M P., Chisholm, K J & Cockshott, W P. "Problems with persistent programming langauges"/ presented at the Workshop on programming languages and database systems, University of Pennsylvania. October 1982. Circulated (revised) in the Workkshop proceedings 1983, see PERSISTENT PROGRAMMING RESEARCH REPORT-2-83.

Atkinson, M P. "Data management". in Encyclopedia of Computer Science and Engineering 2nd Edition, Ralson & Meek (editors) January 1983. van Nostrand Reinhold.

Atkinson, M P., Chisholm, K J & Cockshott, W P. "Algorithms for a Persistent Heap". Software Paractice and Experience, Vol. 13. No.3. 259-272 (March 1983). Also as EUCS Departmental Report CSR-109-82.

Atkinson, M P., Chisholm, K J & Cockshott, W P. "CMS - A chunk management system". Software Practice and Experience, Vol.13, No.3. (March 1983) 273-185. Also as ECUS Departmental Report CSR-110-82.

Atkinson, M P., Bailey, P J., Chisholm, K J., Cockshott, W P. & Morrison, R. "Current progress with persistent programming". presented at the DEC workshop on Programing Languages and Databases. Boston, April 1983.

BIBLIOGRAPHY

Atkinson, N P., Bailey, J P., Chisholm, K J, Cockshott, W P & Morrison, R. "An approach to persistent programming" The Computer Journal, 1983, Vol. 26, No.4. 360-365 - see PERSISTENT PROGRAMMING RESEARCH REPORT 2-83.

Atkinson, M P., Bailey P J., Chisholm, K J., Cockshott W P. & Morrison, R. "PS-algol a language for persistent programming". 10th Australian Computer Conference, Melbourne, Sept. 1983, 70-79 - see PERSISTENT PROGRAMMING RESEARCH REPORT 2-83.

Morrison, R., Weatherill, M., Podolski Z and Bailey, P J. "High level language support for 3-dimension graphics" . Eurographics Conference Zagreb, North Holland, 7-17, Sept. 1983 (ed. PJ W ten Hagen)

Cockshott, W P., Atkinson, M P., Chisholm, K J., Bailey, P J & Morrison, R. "POMS: a persistent object management system", Software Practice & Experience, Vol. 14, No.1, 49-71, January 1984.

Kulkarni, K G & Atkinson, M P. "Experimenting with the Functional Data Model", in Databases - Role and Structure, Cambridge University Press, Cambridge, England, 1984.

Atkinson, M P & Morrison, R. "Persistent First Class Procedures are Enough", Foundations of Software Technology and Theoretical Computer Science (ed. M Joseph & R shyamasundar) Lecture Notes in Computer Science 181, Springer Verlag, Brlin (1984).

Atkinson, M P., Bocca, J B ., Elsey T J., Fiddian N J., Flower, M., Gray, P M D., Gray W P., Hepp, P E., Johnson R G., Milne W., Norrie M C., Omolou A O., Oxborrow E A., Shave M J R., Smith A M., Stocker P M., & Walker, J. "The Proteus distributed database system" proceedings of the third British National Conference on Databases (ed. J Longstaff), BCS Workshop Series, Cambridge University Press, Cambridge, England (July 1984).

Atkinson M P & Morrison R. "Procedures as persistent data objects" ACM TOPLAS 7, 4, 539-559 (Oct.1985) - see PERSISTENT PROGRAMMING RESEARCH REPORT-9-84.

Morrison R, Bailey P J., Dearle A., Brown P & Arkinson M P. "The persistent store as an enabling technology for integrated support environments" 8th International Conference on Software Engineering, Imperial College, London (August 1985) 166-172 - see PERSISTENT PROGRAMMING RESEARCH REPORT-15-85.

Atkinson M P & Morrison R. "Types, bindings and parameters in a persistent environment" proceedings of Data Types and Persistence Workshop, Appin, August 1985, 1-24, - see PERSISTENT PROGRAMMING RESEARCH REPORT-16-85

Davie, J T. "Conditional declaration and pattern matching" proceedings of Data Types and Persistencve Workshop, Appin, August 1985, 278-283 - see PERSISTENT PROGRAMMING RESEARCH REPORT-16-85.

Krablin, G L., "Building flexible multilevel transactions in a distributed persistent environment, proceedings of Data Types and Persistence Workshop, Appin, August 1985, 86-117 - see PERSISTENT PROGRAMMING RESEARCH REPORT-16-85.

Buneman, O P., "Data types for data base programming", proceedings of Data Types and Persistence Workshop, Appin, August 1985, 291-303 - see PERSISTENT PROGRAMMING RESEARCH REPORT-16-85

Cockshott, W P., "Addressing mechanisms and persistent programming", proceedings of Data Types and Persistence Workshop, Appin, August 1985, 363-383 - see PERSISTENT PROGRAMMING RESEARCH REPORT-16-85

Norrie, M C. "Addressing mechanisms and persistent programming", proceedings of Data Types and Persistence Workshop, Appin, August 1985, 363-383 - see PERSISTENT PROGRAMMING RESEARCH REPORT-16-85.

Owoso, G O. "On the need for a flexible Type System in Persistent Programming Languages", proceedings of Data Types and Persistence Workshop, Appin, August 1985, 423-438 - see PERSISTENT PROGRAMMING RESEARCH REPORT-16-85.

Morrison, R., Brown, A L., Bailey, P J., Davie, A J T & Dearle, A. "A persistent graphics facility for the ICL PERQ", Software Practice and Experience, Vol.14, No.3 (1986) - see PERSISTENT PROGRAMMING RESEARCH REPORT-10-84

Atkinson, M P and Morrison, R. "Integrated Persistent Programming Systems", proceedings of the 19th Annual Hawaii International Conference on System Sciences, January 7-10, 1986 (ed. B D Shriver), vol IIA, Software 842-854, Western Periodicals Co., 1300 Rayman St. North Holywood, Calif. 91605, USA - see PERSISTENT PROGRAMMING RESEARCH REPORT-19-85

Atkinson M P., Morrison R and Pratten, G D. "A Persistent Information Space Architecture", proceedings of the 9th Australian Computing Science Conference, January 1986 - see PERSISTENT PROGRAMMING RESEARCH REPORT-21-85

Kulkarni, K G & Atkinson, M P. "EFDM: Extended Functional Data Model", The Computer Journal, Vol. 29, No.1 (1986) 38-45.

Buneman, O P & Atkinson, M P. "Inheritance and Persistence in Database Programming Languages" proceedings ACM SIGMOD Conference 1986, Washington, USA May 1986 - see PERSISTENT PROGRAMMING RESEARCH REPORT-22-86.

Morrison R., Dearle A., Brown A., & Atkinson M P. "An integrated graphics programming environment", Computer Graphics Forum, Vol. 5, No.2. June 1986, 147-157 - see PERSISTENT PROGRAMMING RESEARCH REPORT-14-86.

Atkinson, M G., Morrison R & Pratten, G D. "Designing a Persistent Information Space Architecture", proceedings of Information Processing 1986, Dublin, September 1986 (ed H J Kuglet) 115-119, North Holland Press.

Brown, A L & Dearle, A. "Implementation Issues in Persistent Graphics" University Computing Vol. 8 No.2. (Summer 1986) - see PERSISTENT PROGRAMMING RESEARCH REPORT-23-86.

Cockshott, W P, "Persistent programming and secure data storage," Information and Software Technology, Vol 29 pp 249-256, Butterworth, June 1987.

Balch, P, W P Cockshott, and P W Foulk, "Layered implementations of persistent object stores," Software Engineering Journal, pp 123-131, IEE, March 1989

Internal Reports

PERSISTENT PROGRAMMING RESEARCH REPORTS are published by the Computer Science Department of the University of Glasgow.

Morrison, R "S-algol language reference manual", University of St. Andrews CS-79-1, 1979

Bailey, P J., Maritz P & Morrison, R. "The S-algol abstract machine", University of St. Andrews CS-80-2, 1980

Atkinson, M P., Hepp, P E., Ivanov H; McDuff A; Proctor R & Wilson A G. "EDQUSE reference manual" Department of Computer Science, University of Edinburgh September 1981

Hepp, P & Norrie M C. "AQUEL: User Manual" Department of Computer Science Report CSR-188-85, University of Edinburgh

Norrie, M C. "The Edinburgh Node of the Proteus Distributed Database System" Department of Computer Science Reports CSR-191-85 University of Edinburgh.

Brown, A L and W P Cockshott, "CPOMS a revised version of the persistent object management system in C," PERSISTENT PROGRAMMING RESEARCH REPORT 13, 1985

W P Cockshott, "The persistent store machine",PPRR-18,1985

W P Cockshott, "Building a microcomputer with persistent virtual memory," PPRR-20, 1985

W P Cockshott, "Design of POMP - Persistent Object Management coProcessor," Computer Science Research Report, Vol ARCH-1-88, University of Strathclyde, October 1988

W P Cockshott, "S: Persistent Salgol Compiler for the IBM AT," Computer Science Research Report, Vol ARCH-6-89, University of Strathclyde, March 1989

W P Cockshott, "Layered Implementation of a Persistent Object Store," Computer Science Research Report, Vol ARCH-6-89, University of Strathclyde, July 1989

W P Cockshott, "Definition and linkage techniques for graphics abstract datatypes," Computer Science Research Report, Vol ARCH-7-89, University of Strathclyde, November 1989

Theses

W P Cockshott - Orthogonal Persistence, University of Edinburgh, February 1983

K G Kulkarni - Evaluation of Functional Data Models for Database Design and Use, University of Edinburgh 1983

P E Hepp - A DBS Architect Supporting Coexisting Query Langauges and Data Models, University of Edinburgh 1983

G D M Ross - Virtual Files: A Framework for Experiemental Design, University of Edinburgh 1983.

G O Owoso - Data Description and Manipulation in Persistent Programming Languages, University of Edinburgh 1984.

Index

```
! 33
#pixel 51
$ 46
$$int 46
$pntr 46
$string 56
& 48
''' 26
'' 25
'b 26
'n 25
'o 26
'p 26
't 26
( 26
) 26
* 26, 28
**int 42
*int 42
*string 42
+ 26, 28
```

```
++ 28, 76
- 26, 28
.out 115
/ 28
80386 20
: 29, 45
:: 42
:= 30, 31
< 27
<= 27
= 27, 31
> 27
>= 27
? 54
@ 39
abstract machine 59, 60,
   63, 64, 80
abstractions 75
access
   control 18
   speed 93
```

INDEX

address 86, 87, 88
  evaluation 73
addressing modes 71
algebra 76
algol-like 29
Algol 59, 60, 64, 67
  scope rules 33
algol-60 4, 113
Algol68 2, 23, 63, 75, 80
Algols68C 23
algolW 80
algorithm 36
algorithmic maps 35
alien 116
alien procedures 116
analogue computer 5
and 28
approximation 25
arguments 65
arithmetic operators 38
array 14, 18, 67
  of words 65
ASCII 27
assembler 116
assembly language 120
assignment 77
  operations 76
atomic transactions 96
Backus Naur Form 4
base type 24, 84
begin ... end 32
binary tree 67
binder 106, 115, 116, 117
binding mechanism 114
bit 7, 51
bit plane 51
bitmap 50, 82
  vector 83
block 32, 33, 65
  innermost 65
  logical 95, 98
  outermost 65
  relative 95

structure, languages 70, 72
BNF, see Backus Naur Form 4
bool 24, 76
boolean 24, 52
buffer 12
business machines 10
C 2, 13, 14, 15, 60, 61, 62, 70, 80, 81, 99, 104, 113, 116, 117, 120, 122
cache 101
CAD 19, 20, 22
Cartesian
  product 39
    space 38, 42, 43, 47
case 17, 29
cbool 30
character 25
cint 30
circuit schematic 22
class 84, 98
  descriptor 98
  fraction 98, 99
  of 44
    identifiers 45
    pntr 44
    store 63
    variables 71
clause 33
closure 70, 108, 109, 111, 115
COBOL 2, 11
code
  address 71
  pointer 108, 111
  store 64
colour planes 50
combine 47, 48
commit 55, 56, 109
  operation 89
  procedure 90
  time 102
commit.database 92
comparison 28

compile time 42, 84
compiler 31
compound statement 32
computer memory 53
constants 30
context of declaration 108, 113
conventional heap 86
copy ... onto ... 52
copy 52
CPOMS 94, 99, 109
  PID 100
CPU 10, 72
crash 94
creal 30
create 56
create.chunk 92
create.database 55
cstring 30
Data Manipulation Language 15
data processing 10
data structures 15
database 11, 15, 17, 18, 20, 56, 89, 94, 99
  management 54
  relational 22
datafile 100
dators 10
DBMS 15, 17, 18
DEC Vax 63
declaration 47
default 29, 45
degrees 50
device 50
digital
  computer 6
  store 6
dimension 52
disk 10, 17, 23, 53, 89, 90, 91, 93, 98
  address 101
  block 97
  organisation 93
  storage 18

store 11
display 72
div 28
division by zero 37
DML see Data Manipulation Language 15
dyadic 26, 27
dynamic
  binder 114, 121
  link 71
  linker 116
  linking 113, 122
Edinburgh University 19
effective address 72
elements 39, 42
empty set 38
engineering 19
enumerated types 18
environment 72
  variable 115
epsilon 27
Euclidean space 76
expression 26
ext 104
external 105, 106, 114
  library 104
false 24, 26, 28
fieldname 84
file 11, 12, 13, 14, 50, 53, 54, 55, 56, 86
  closing 54
  opening 54
  variable 12
filing systems 18
finite state automaton 7
first class function 33, 67, 99, 103, 108, 113
first line of program 114
floppy disks 10
for .. to... by .. do 32
FORTRAN 2, 62, 104
frame 72
FSA see finite state automaton 9

FTOS see floating point
top of stack 66
functional 34
garbage collection 78, 80, 81, 89
garbage collector 112
get 12
get.chunk 92
get.size 92
global 65, 72
   variable 109
grammar 25
graph structure 53
graphics types 47
grid 51
hard disks 10
hardware 37
   interpretation 59, 62
Harvard machines 9
hash table 91
hashing 89
heap 63, 64, 78, 85, 89, 94
   allocation 112
   conventional 86
   manager 115
   object 109
   persistent 77, 91
   RAM 95
heap, volatile 77, 78, 79, 80, 91
high 28
high level languages 17
horizontal axis 39
IBM PC 34, 63
IBM PC AT 45
ICL Perq 63
identifier 30, 45
if ... then ... else 17
Iliffe vectors 96
image ... by ... of ... 51
image 51, 52, 76, 77, 82
   object 83
IMP 60

import clause 114
include 54
index 42, 52, 89
   file 100, 101, 102
input devices 11
input output primitives 32
int 24, 76
integer 24, 27, 31
Intel 117
intelligent compiler 113
intermediate scope 70
intialization 31
invisible procedures 116
is 28
isnt 28
ISO character strings 76
ISO standard Pascal 13
ISPS 64, 65, 72
join 47, 48
jump chain 116
Last In First Out 64
left hand side 40
let 30, 33, 40
lexical level 72
lexicographic ordering 67
library segment 114, 116
limit 52
linker 106
Linn Products 63
   Rekursiv 117
Lisp 80
list 13, 18
   of cons cells 54
literal 24, 25, 26, 33
local 72
   variables 69
location 31
lock 100
logical
   block 98
   disk address 96
   space 96
longevity of data 19

lookup table 43, 96
loops 32
low 28
lower bound 83
LR.map 95, 96, 97, 98
lwb 42
M68000 61, 63
macro expansion 59, 60
main stack 109
map 35, 36, 38
  algorithmic 35, 43
  application of 35
  from string to type 45
  identifier to value 44
  partial 37, 44
  predefined 52
  storage 35, 43, 37
    partial 44
mapping 78, 91
  total 36
maxint 24
microcode 63
  interpretation 59, 61
microcode interpretation 61
microprocessor 15
minus 26
mode 75
modular compilation 103
modules 18
monadic 26
mouse bios 122
MS see main stack
MSDOS 54, 56
multiply 49
nand 52
negative area 37
nested procedures 113
nets 21
neural network 5
nil 45, 46
non volatile 93, 94
non-void 29
NOP instruction 121

nor 52
NOS see next of stack
not 26, 52
  see ~
nullfile 56
numerals 41
object 76, 78, 89, 90, 95
  creation 93
  image 83
  on heap 81
  semantics 75, 76
  size of 99
  vector 77
OBJEKT 63
of 29
off 51
offset 69, 72
on 51
open 56
open.database 55, 92
operating system 12, 87
operator 26
or 28
order of evaluation 26, 28
origin 50
output 54
  devices 11
P stack 77, 78, 79, 80, 81
p-code 59
paradigms 1
parameter 70
partial map 44
partition 99, 100
  data file 101
Pascal 11, 12, 13, 14, 20, 22, 26, 29, 54, 59, 80, 86
password 100
performance ladder 61
persistence, orthogonal 53
persistent

database 91
heap 77, 91
IDentifier 86, 87
names 12
Object Management System 94
   see also POMS
Pascal 23
programming 17
  language 24
store 33, 108
pic 47, 50, 76, 77
picture 47
PID 86, 87, 88, 89, 91, 95, 96, 99, 101
Pidlam 89
Pidlam 90
pixel 50, 51, 52
pixel mapping 52
plane 51
plane geometry 47
pntr 44, 77, 99
  class of 44
  value 56
point 39
pointer 18, 77, 80, 81
  comparison 85
  dereference 84
polyadic 29
polymorphism 84
POMS 94, 95, 96, 98, 109
portability 61
postfix notation 65
prameter passing 33
prameters 38
priorities 28
proc 33, 37
procedure 33, 36, 38
  calls 67
  header 116
  variables 34
PROCNAME 120
program 10
programming language 11, 15, 18, 19, 35, 53, 59

projection 39
PS-algol - origins 19
PSDIR 115
PSF 77
PSP 77
psr 120, 117
PTODI 101, 102
public sector borrowing requirement 39
put 12
put.chunk 92
quote 25
RAM 12, 17, 86, 89, 93, 98, 106, 108
RAM see Read Write Random Access Memory 9
rand 52
random access
  devices 12
  store 9, 63
RAS see random access store 9
raster graphics 50
rasterop 52
read 13
Read Only Memory 9
Read Write Random Access Memory 9
read.a.line 56
read.r 31
read.r 32
readi 56
real 24, 25, 27, 37, 76
real number line 38
records 18
recursive 64
  grammar 64
referential transparency 30
register 64
relation 18, 89
relational database 22
rem 28
repeat ... while 32
representation 24

reset 12
return address 71
rewrite 12
RGB 50
RISC 62
ROM see Read Only Memory 9
root table 91
ror 52
rotate 50
run time 42, 84
  binder 114
  system 55
s 117
S-algol 23, 24, 42, 53, 104
s-code 59, 63, 65
s.enter 55, 56
s.lookup 55, 56
Salgol syntax 34
sb 106
scale operator 49
scan lines 83
schema 18
scope 64
  rules 12, 18
scope rules 18
screen 51, 83
secondary storage 10
seek 13
segment 114, 115
  directive 113
selection operation 29
self describing 81
semantics
  object 75, 76
  value 75
sequential file 11
Series 39 63
set 18, 35, 38
  empty 38, 45
  finite 44
  of identifiers 44, 45
  of points 47
SF 70, 70, 77

register 72
SF register see stack frame
shadow paging 94
shift 49
Smalltalk 63
SOAR 63
software
  interpretation 59, 60
  interrupt 117
SP 70, 77
SP register see stack pointer 65
space
  dimension 39
  logical 96
speed 98
SQL 15
sqrt 33
square of 36
St Andrews University 23
stack 63, 64, 67, 110
  allocation 112
  frame 65, 109
  object 110, 111
  pointer 65
  main 65
state 6, 9, 76
  vector 9
statement 31, 32
static link 71, 72, 108, 109, 111
storage
  claim 78
  locations 30, 41
  maps 35, 43
  recovery 80
  release 78
store 2, 31, 63
  instruction 65
  object 75
string 18, 24, 25, 27, 28, 67, 76, 77, 81, 99
  comparison 67
  constant 45

INDEX

structure 44, 76, 77, 84, 85
  class 55, 85
structure of memory 63
substring 27, 39
syntax 35
tab ... of 45
table 45, 56
terminate 10
top 87
TOS 66
TOS see top of stack 66
trademark 84
transaction 94
  abort 94
  atomic 96
  commit 94
  start 94
transformations 49
  geometric 49
triadic operators 29
true 24, 26, 28
tuple 89
Turbo Pascal 13
two pass compiler 113
type 21
  checking 55, 84
  definition 17
  sequence of 38
  specification 33
  system 24
typing 15
union 87
Unix 13, 15, 55, 100
Unix Ps-algol tables 56
upb 42
update 76
upper bound 83
User ID 100
value 30, 31, 33, 51
  semantics 75
variables, scalar 59
Vax 61
  machine code 60
  VMS 34

VDU 12
vector 38, 39, 42, 47, 76, 83, 99
  assignment 40
  constancy 40
  Iliffe 96
  object 77
  space 40, 43
  type 43
  variables 77
  bitmap 83
  indices 42
  values 41
viewport 50
volatile heap 77, 78, 79, 80, 91, 102
Von Neumann 2, 9, 14
while ... do 31
window 52
windowing packages 12
wire 7, 22
write 13, 31, 32
x.dim 52
xnor 52
xor 52
y.dim 52
z80 15
[39
] 39
^ 12, 48
{ 32
| 52
} 32
~ 26
~= 27

ELLIS HORWOOD SERIES IN COMPUTERS AND THEIR APPLICATIONS
Series Editor: IAN CHIVERS, The Computer Centre, King's College, London, and formerly Senior Programmer and Analyst, Imperial College of Science and Technology, University of London

Rubin, T.	USER INTERFACE DESIGN FOR COMPUTER SYSTEMS
Rudd, A.S.	PRACTICAL USAGE OF ISPF DIALOG MANAGER
de Saram, H.	PROGRAMMING IN MICRO-PROLOG
Savic, D. & Goodsell, D.	APPLICATIONS PROGRAMMING WITH SMALLTALK/V
Schirmer, C.	PROGRAMMING IN C FOR UNIX
Schofield, C.F.	OPTIMIZING FORTRAN PROGRAMS
Sharp, J.A.	DATA FLOW COMPUTING
Sherif, M.A.	DATABASE PROJECTS
Smith & Sage	EDUCATION AND THE INFORMATION SOCIETY
Smith, J.M & Stutely, R.	SGML
Späth, H.	CLUSTER ANALYSIS ALGORITHMS
Späth, H.	CLUSTER DISSECTION AND ANALYSIS
Stratford-Collins, P.	ADA
Tizzard, K.	C FOR PROFESSIONAL PROGRAMMERS
Turner, S.J.	AN INTRODUCTION TO COMPILER DESIGN
Wexler, J.	CONCURRENT PROGRAMMING IN OCCAM 2
Whiddett, R.J.	CONCURRENT PROGRAMMING FOR SOFTWARE ENGINEERS
Whiddett, R.J., Berry, R.E., Blair, G.S., Hurley, P.N., Nicol, P.J., Muir, S.J.	UNIX
Yannakoudakis, E.J. & Hutton, P.J.	SPEECH SYNTHESIS AND RECOGNITION SYSTEMS
Zech, R.	FORTH

Computer Communications and Networking

Currie, W.S.	LANS EXPLAINED
Deasington, R.J.	A PRACTICAL GUIDE TO COMPUTER COMMUNICATIONS AND NETWORKING, 2nd Edition
Deasington, R.J.	X.25 EXPLAINED, 2nd Edition
Henshall, J. & Shaw, S.	OSI EXPLAINED
Kauffels, F.-J.	PRACTICAL LANS ANALYSED
Kauffels, F.-J.	PRACTICAL NETWORKS ANALYSED
Kauffels, F.-J.	UNDERSTANDING DATA COMMUNICATIONS
Muftic, S.	SECURITY MECHANISMS FOR COMPUTER NETWORKS

$27.50

UNIVERSITY OF MAINE

RAYMOND H. FOGLER LIBRARY